A Teacher's Notebook
Stories from the Sixties

By Frederick Kuri

Copyright ©2017 by Frederick Kuri

Cover Design by Davies Associates, Inc.
Interior Design by Pamela Morrell

ISBN: 978-0-9995488-1-3

All rights reserved. No part of this book may be reproduced in any form or by any electronic or mechanical means without permission, in writing, from Dragon Tree Books.

Published by

1620 SW 5th Avenue
Pompano Beach, Florida 33060
(954)788-4775
editors@editingforauthors.com
dragontreebooks.com

Contents

Preface v

Gathering Dust 1

Home of the Brave 25

Christina 55

About the Author 73

Preface

Rarely in the relationship between student and teacher is one marked for life. Nonetheless, under the extraordinary circumstances of the classroom extraordinary relationships form leaving impressions that linger with the reach of time. More than forty years have slipped by since the encounters these stories return to, years with their change in perspective which enlarges the remembrance.

Pride in those days found expression without self-importance. Loyalty, staying power, a willingness to sacrifice for another were commonplace among the working poor. No one conceived of entitlement, either for schools or individuals. There were no victims, and convenience played little part in determining priorities. Burdens were shouldered because there seemed no other way or because one cared passionately. The classroom, where individual responsibility was requisite, proved a harsh testing ground, and not solely for the student.

What a privilege to have worked with those who stood firmly, to have for a brief time witnessed their trials and through them had a glimpse of the higher qualities of our, at times, all too human nature. For those remarkable individuals these stories were written.

Gathering Dust

October 1964 was no different than other years. Strong Santa Ana winds from the Mojave Desert moved west through the San Gabriel Mountains and swept the broad Los Angeles basin to the sea. Hot autumn days were the result which ended in balmy sunsets over the Pacific Ocean. Breaching the flat city landscape, the Hollywood Hills were refreshed by the wind and exquisite sunset vistas. Residents of the quiet hillside homes where autumn leaves were turning as usual had no reason for concern with the streets of South Central or their schools. One might have called them carefree days when Marty Hatton began teaching—the tree-lined canyons where he had grown up were never squeezed by too many people. City Hall was the one landmark permanent above the skyline. Only with darkness did the vast energy below, pulsing through endless roadways to the horizon and beyond, betray itself to the serenity of the hills. As if to give assurance, the great inner city sparkled at night from those hills. The Watts riot did not erupt during that fall season. Not until the following summer did it become apparent that something in the community was very wrong.

I

Classes were out for the seven hundred black children of Eighty-Second Street School though not everyone wanted to go home on a windy and hot

Friday afternoon. The yard attendant would soon arrive to release equipment so the restless youngsters who lingered on the playground or in the shade near the equipment lockers could play. Those roaming aimlessly along the sidewalk beside the strong chain-link fence suddenly began to shout and to run. Others waiting nearby on the playground noticed and immediately gave chase. Before long all the children were running in the same direction.

Inside Bungalow G which stood alone at the far end of the playground Marty made final rounds to straighten chairs, pick up pencils and forgotten papers. The term had hardly begun and already he was exhausted. Every day was a struggle with his pupils for control, and each week he felt increasingly alone. He was learning that inner-city children were more likely to get into a fight than to take notice of anything he would say. This small elementary school was nothing like those he had attended as a child. After six weeks, everyone remained a stranger.

Perspiration stood out on his forehead as he snatched a jacket from a familiar chair at the back. "Never think about tomorrow," he muttered with frustration in the stifling room and flung the jacket over a hook in the cloakroom. "Hot afternoons have nothing to do with cold mornings." He stopped along the side aisle to close and lock the windows but failed to notice the deserted school yard. Marty had not yet learned that an empty playground immediately after school meant trouble.

He returned to his cluttered desk, wondering what he could do that would make a difference. He had given short assignments for the ten-year-olds to complete at home. But that had proved unrealistic. Both papers and books went missing. Some had never done homework, he realized. Then a parent complained and the principal told him to assign no more than fifteen minutes a couple of times a week. *What good is that?* he asked and was reminded that learning was to be emphasized while in the classroom. The freshman teacher felt more unsure than ever.

He glanced at the clock on the wall. Friday meant another faculty meeting. He grabbed a stack of papers from his double-pedestaled desk and one by one pinned them on the bulletin board. Displaying the childrens' best work would be an encouragement, he hoped. But teaching fifth graders was not what he had expected. Most of his energy was spent maintaining order. Conflicts, both boys and girls, were continuous and inevitably ended with a fight. He did not understand raw aggression in a ten-year-old, aggression that was not only disturbing to him but unfamiliar from his own childhood.

Marty put up the last paper, glanced again at the clock on the wall, drew a deep breath to relieve the knot in the pit of his stomach and wiped his forehead. He locked the big desk before leaving.

A wide playground separated the bungalow from the main buildings, and Marty moved with long strides over the worn asphalt. Walking helped him relax. The empty playing field reminded him of the summer day when he first drove into South Central to interview for the fifth grade position. The heat had been oppressive and he recalled being startled by the neighborhood of small houses that surrounded the school. Rusting automobiles were parked in front yards where no children played. Only a couple of stray dogs on the street, and nothing maintained—houses, dogs or automobiles. But tall palm trees greeted him at the school grounds, and the low stucco buildings were interconnected by covered corridors. The principal, a short man dressed in a dark three-piece suit, looked like a banker and was introduced as Mr. D. "Used to be a nice little neighborhood," Mr. D. reminisced. He gestured toward the playground, "Grass, trees. All changed now. A quiet little school—a country club, Hatton." As they crossed the asphalt on their way to the fifth-grade bungalow, Marty questioned the high fences excluding the palm trees from the school yard. "Experience," was the curt reply. "Takes experience to work the inner city." Mr. D. said little else that day before approving Marty for the vacant fifth grade position. Now as Marty crossed the playground, he no longer noticed the palm trees or the high fences but wondered why he had been given an assignment that demanded experience.

He reached the shade of the main building, turned the corner toward the faculty room door and stopped short. The vacant knoll behind the teacher's parking lot was teeming with children. Without thinking, he bolted along the sidewalk past books and notebooks left behind, papers ripped by eager feet now blowing loose on the pavement. He leapt over a low brick wall that lined the parking area and stumbled when he started up the dusty hill. A couple of stragglers laughed aloud as he picked himself up and rushed into the hive of children. "Break it up!" he called out, pushing youngsters aside. "Everyone go home!" But no one responded. At the top, two bigger boys circled one another with fists held close to their faces. Three others stood in the clearing.

Marty broke through the final barrier of spectators as the taller of the two combatants struck out, catching his adversary's shirt. The smaller boy dodged back, his shirt tearing as he moved. Although the fist missed its mark, the youngster lost balance and fell against the dirt. Instantly he sprang to his haunches and faced his antagonist. The torn shirt hung open, revealing a slender, panting chest. The children pressed closer. The tall boy was winning.

Marty was momentarily stunned by the number of children on the hill. Half the school surrounded him. What would he do if the fight spread? He glanced around. No teachers were in sight. Where was Mr. D.? But he spotted one of his boys, Willy Brown, as the child slipped from behind the front row of legs on the opposite side of the clearing and said something to the boy on the ground. Marty moved quickly, seizing the tall boy's arm. "That's enough!" His voice cut the tense silence. The youth did not resist his firm grasp. He was slender, nearly as tall as Marty and beads of sweat stood out on his clear, mahogany, boyish face. Even while motionless, he seemed graceful.

"Come on, man," urged one of the three standing nearby. "You got the dude, man. He ain't goin' mess no more!" The three moved into the crowd as the children fell back, opening a path.

"Can't you talk when there's a problem?" Marty blurted out, but the tall boy jerked his arm free and without a sideward glance slipped into the mass of awed children. The youngster left alone in the clearing spat at the four who had turned their backs on him then stalked off down the hill and did not respond to smaller boys who shadow-boxed in his direction from a safe distance.

The young teacher searched the swarm of disappointed youngsters for some sign of recognition. And there was Willy Brown. "William!" he called out, but the child kept moving down the hill with the others. "William Hamilton Brown!" Marty bellowed. "You hear me talking to you!"

The ten-year-old stopped, a sullen resentment coloring his expression. He mumbled something but did not turn to his teacher. A group of boys stood by as Marty approached. "Who were those guys?"

"I ain't see nobody." Willy stared hard at the dirt.

"You were speaking to one of them." The boy's sullen resentment stopped Marty. *I'm your teacher and you don't trust me*, he realized. The boy continued to look away in silence.

"Your jacket's in the room," Marty said finally, his tone softened. "I liked the paragraph you wrote with the spelling words. I put your paper on the board." The youngster turned but made no reply. "Okay," Marty said quietly, "you go on home."

He watched the boy move silently down the hill. As the children turned toward home, he felt a wave of relief and shaded his eyes from the sun. The fight was over and no one had been hurt. "Don't forget your notebooks!" he shouted with effort, his throat parched from the desert wind. Typical of October, the day was warmer than mid-summer.

Marty ran the last few yards toward school and hurdled the wall behind the teachers' parking lot, left leg forward, as he had done with his high school track team. One of the fifth grade boys watched his new teacher in amazement, then applauded. Marty waved as he sprinted to the faculty room and quickly pulled open the door. The knot in his stomach was gone.

"Hatton!" exclaimed the figure in a dark three-piece suit seated at one end of the narrow room. Smoke gushed through Mr. D's teeth as he fingered an enormous cigar. "Meeting at three-twenty," he grumbled. Eighteen teachers were sitting around several tables.

"Fight on the hill," Marty replied, catching his breath as he entered the crowded room.

"Meeting at three-twenty," the principal repeated with an edge of irritation. "These ladies want to get home."

"Junior high boys," Casey Church, one of the sixth grade teachers, droned from the far corner. "Happens all the time."

Mr. D. stood up, his slight figure leaning toward a sheaf of papers in his hand. "I've spoken to the junior high about those boys." He cleared his throat before the hushed teachers.

"Remember last year?" Church grumbled. "Every damned Friday. Like clockwork." He turned to Marty. "No good closing the gate after the horse is out, old buddy."

Marty took the only empty chair. "One of my boys knows something," he remarked, glancing around at the others. Mr. D. removed an immaculate handkerchief from his coat pocket and began to clean his glasses. Marty turned in confusion to the others. "Didn't you see them fighting?" No one responded.

The principal put on his glasses, again cleared his throat and turned to one of the black women at the front. "What basal reader do you fourth grade teachers want for next term?"

A thin column of smoke rose from the cigar, furled upon itself and wafted invisibly, filling the tiny room with an acrid, quickly stale aroma. The routine had begun. The new teacher shifted his position. Once more he was gripped by the knot in the pit of his stomach, but as he stared ahead the fight on the hill came to mind blocking out the meeting. He had never before touched black skin and had assumed that, like leather, it was rough. He now recalled the tall boy's arm. The skin was soft.

II

Monday morning Eighty-Second Street School was sealed under a grey, moist fog. The room lights went on and off as the janitor made his rounds, opening blinds and turning on heaters before staff arrived. Marty was early and went directly to the main building to sign in, but when he reached the counter, Mr. D. darted from his office. "Your room's a shamble," he uttered with a violent tremble. The new teacher stared at him without comprehending. "School police on the way. Come on."

They left the building. "Give 'em schools. What for? Tear the place apart. Tear it apart, I tell you!" The principal moved with quick, agitated steps across the asphalt. "Used to know them all. And the mothers. A country club, Hatton! Now look around. Six, eight, ten to a family. Don't even know the father's name! Five years ago there wasn't one here." They reached Bungalow G. "Stay out of fights," the staccato voice rasped. "Stirs things up!" Mr. D. unlocked the door and entered. In the flat morning light he righted a chair and feverishly began picking up books from the rubble.

Marty stared in disbelief. There was a ragged hole in one window where the glass had been shattered and the venetian blinds torn apart to admit the vandals. Yellow paint ran down the walls in long streaks, forming globs on the floor that were thick with the papers and books of what had been his classroom. "What time is the assembly?" he asked finally, his voice dry and shaken.

Mr. D. stopped abruptly. "No assembly!" He thumped the pile of books he had rescued. "Use the auditorium. Maintenance will be here. Should have your room back in a couple of days."

"You don't talk to them?" Marty could hardly form the words.

"Junior high boys. No assembly." He pounded the books. "Hands tied. Kids don't care."

"But the parents?"

"Junior high boys, I tell you." He brushed past Marty. "Use the auditorium, Hatton!" He released the open door and disappeared outside.

The door closed slowly, gradually excluding the pale morning light and finally snapped shut. Marty stood paralyzed, his first classroom destroyed and he was supposed to get up in front of the children as though nothing had happened. A sense of panic began to overtake him. He felt sick to his stomach, but he must do something. Quickly he switched on the lights and crossed to the bulletin board where he had put up their papers. Dry paint obliterated the awkward handwriting, the short, choppy sentences—the best his fifth grade boys and girls could produce. This was how their work was treated, and the principal would do nothing about it. Where was their confidence to come from? The feeling of panic began to give way to a rising anger at the vandals who had broken into the classroom and at the system that would tolerate such behavior. He crossed the room with unexpected determination, kicked over the chair Mr. D. had righted and grabbed the big desk. He slammed it onto its legs then went back and picked up the chair he had kicked over. No one to distinguish right from wrong. Indifference. The attitude fueled his anger, though he knew anger would not make things better for the children. The reality of their world was beginning to engulf him. He felt as though he himself were drowning.

A few moments later the bungalow door closed behind him as he walked rapidly toward the auditorium. He carried an English text, a torn speller and an arithmetic book. There was no time to think. He had to get organized. If the children were not kept busy, the day would be a nightmare of temperament and chaos.

The warning bell rang and Marty left the auditorium. The children on the playground were lining up to walk to class. He noticed Willy Brown watching him as he went into a noisy group of fourth graders and made them straighten their line and stand silently before a substitute teacher. *Mr. Hatton's in a bad mood!* caught his ear as he approached his own class line. Marty greeted the children at the front and wondered if any of them dreaded the day as much as he.

When the children entered the auditorium, instead of a projector at the back for films, there was a portable blackboard at the front, and instead of sitting where they pleased, Marty placed them in the front rows with an empty seat between each child. He began immediately with arithmetic. Willy Brown managed to sit in the farthest row back where he could draw pictures on his paper.

It was nearly time for recess when their papers were collected, and Marty waited beside a table at the front he was using for a desk while the class settled. He could not go on as though nothing had happened. "Some of you were at the fight last Friday," he began, looking directly at those he had seen on the hill. "When I tell you to break it up, you don't hang around!" The auditorium echoed the teacher's voice and fell silent. Marty shot a quick glance at the clock. The big hand clicked—three minutes to recess.

"When I tell you to clear away from a fight," he repeated emphatically, "you walk away without a word!" He rapped his hand sharply on the table. "Walk away without a word! Is that clear?" The echo had hardly died in the large hall before one of the boys on the aisle bounced up and started toward the door. "Claiborne!" Marty cried out.

"I ain't say nothin'," the wiry child replied in a high-pitched voice, and with a quick grin danced around in a circle before flopping back into his seat. Willy laughed aloud and appeared ready to follow Claiborne's example, but Marty moved forward so quickly that everyone hushed.

Again he glanced at the clock. One minute to go. "Any more clowning like that, Mr. Claiborne, and you won't have recess!"

"Mista Claiborne," someone mimicked in a loud whisper, and the teacher turned to see who had spoken.

"Mista Claiborne," someone else repeated, and again he turned, but the big hand moved forward and the passing bell rang.

A few minutes before the warning bell would signal the end of recess, Marty entered the small faculty room. "Say, old buddy," Church's voice boomed out, "that's some party they had in your room. Damned shame!" Marty poured himself a cup of coffee. "Of course," the big teacher continued paternally, "I'd think it over before I broke up any more fights." He glanced knowingly at the others.

Marty walked to one side and sat down. "But it's our job to break up fights. They don't know any better."

"The hell they don't! They do what their brothers and sisters do. Look who y'all dealing with, old buddy, for Christ's sake!"

"Who am I dealing with, for Christ's sake? You tell me!" Marty's hands were trembling. "They're children!"

"Off school grounds—you're not paid to be a cop!"

"They're children!" Marty turned in desperation to the only black teacher present. "Odessa, don't you want something better for them?"

"You're right, Mr. Hatton, honey," she replied firmly. "But I don't like folks shouting and swearing where they can hear. They get enough at home and they're right outside there, and you two don't make no difference shouting at each other. Sure we got to tell them, honey. I tells them every day in my room, and they better listen to me."

"That's what I say," Church retorted, "inside the classroom."

The morning was growing warm as the sun burned through the ground fog, but the windows of the tiny faculty room would remain shut. There was enough confusion in the school without the teachers' only rest area becoming a receptacle for the erratic outbursts of several hundred black children and the thirty or forty odd stragglers from the neighborhood of the country club days. Even with the windows closed, the shouting, the flaring tempers reached them through the very pores of the walls. There was no escape but to close one's mind to it all. Marty had to clear his head so he could accomplish something with the children. Nearly five hours of the day remained.

A few years before, according to Mr. D., there had been nine teachers in the school. The border of the large playground had been open and green and planted with trees where the pupils could eat lunch on the grass, picnic fashion. But now those trees were replaced by bungalows and what had been a shady carpet was dirty asphalt, broken at the edges and painted over with lines for hopscotch and four square. Before the population shift, with its influx of poor black families from the South seeking work, there were no high fences or bungalows to crowd the playground. Marty looked up from his coffee cup. Even the faculty room which had been adequate for nine would have to do for nineteen.

"That's too bad about your room, Mr. Hatton," Odessa said as she moved to sit across from Marty. "Last year they got my room. And, honey, I was supposed to go on teaching! Why, I went home to my husband in tears every night after that. To do such a thing! I worried myself sick expecting it again."

"But how do we teach respect?" Marty asked. "When I see that stone wall in their eyes, I feel I don't belong here. They're telling me it's none of my business. But it is my business. It should be everybody's business. How else can we make a difference?"

"Thank you for helping this morning," the substitute said as she joined them. "Such restless fourth graders. No wonder their teacher is ill. I hope the older ones are better behaved."

"Y'all miss the point, ma'am," Church responded. "Nine-year-old, eleven-year-old. They do what the older ones do. Look who y'all dealing with!"

Mr. D. entered the room. "Hatton," he said hoarsely, "Starr's class is out on a field trip. Said you could have her room. Number six at the end of the hall."

"Second grade classroom?" Marty asked in surprise.

"Second grade. And keep 'em out of the cabinets."

III

At the recess bell, teachers made their separate ways through the hectic movement to where class lines were forming. Some youngsters appeared to go in all directions as if determined by their sheer activity that the passing bell, which signaled the inevitable walk back to class, might never again ring. The playground seemed to converge on itself as Marty was jostled left and right. Complaints from the quiet ones who wanted to stand at the front and be first in line but were displaced by aggressive classmates punctuated the frantic air. The last to leave the games were the first to claim whatever they wanted. Marty had quickly learned that to acknowledge even a single grievance meant a bombardment from every direction and he would accomplish little in getting the children settled. It was his habit to look for stragglers in the rest room.

"I gonna kill that girl!" reached his ears above the general din. He turned to the drinking fountains and there little Willy Brown, shaking with anger, was standing alone. "Nobody say that!" he cried out, unaware of his teacher's presence, and struck his fist against the wall. "I gonna kill that girl!" Tears were streaming down his cheeks.

"William Brown!" Marty said as he approached. "You hear me talking to you!"

"I don' care," the child replied. "Nobody say that!"

"Nobody says what?"

"I don' know." His chest heaved with emotion.

Marty leaned closer to the child. The anguish in his eyes softened Marty's tone. The boy was not simply talking big as they often did over little slights. "What did she say?" Marty asked.

"She make fun o' me. She done it in front o' them girls." He pointed to one of the lines. "She done it Friday, and I don' do nothin'!"

Marty led him past the noisy lines onto the playground. Like most of the children, Willy was not particularly good in class. In fact, he seldom completed an assignment. If he made a mistake, he would throw his pencil in a fit of anger and give up. Until the recent paragraph he had written with the spelling words, Marty could find no reason for the boy to take pride in his work.

"Who made fun of you?" he asked again when they were apart from the others. Marty leaned close to the child. "I'm not going to tell anyone, Willy. You have my promise on that."

"Lydia!" the boy burst out. "She call me ugly!" He wiped his tears roughly with one small fist.

"The redhead? That tall fourth grader in Miss Ritchie's class?"

He shook his head in agreement. "No girl call me ugly!"

"I don't think you're ugly."

"She laugh!" Willy turned away.

"Do you want trouble because of her?"

"No girl call me ugly!"

"Let's find out if she meant it."

"I don' talk to no girl!"

The passing bell rang and classes filed toward their rooms. Marty motioned his class to wait while he and Willy walked to Miss Ritchie's bungalow nearby. He knew Lydia. She was taller than Willy and one of the few white children still attending the school. Lydia took one look at Mr. Hatton with Willy beside him and burst into tears. "You made fun of Willy in front of your girlfriends?" Marty asked sharply. "Willy's mad now. Says he's going to get you. Is that what you want? You're going to fight him after school?"

"No, sir," she replied in a frightened voice.

"If you have something to say, you'd better say it to Willy."

She turned to Miss Ritchie for reassurance though Miss Ritchie was not pleased. "I don't expect you to be rude," she said quietly but with firmness. Willy looked up at the sound of the woman's soft, unfamiliar voice. "Lydia, do you have something to tell us?"

"No, ma'am. I was only kidding."

"Is that all you can say to this young man?" She glanced at Willy who had not taken his eyes from her teacher.

"I'm sorry," Lydia admitted. "I didn't really mean it."

"Do you accept her apology, dear?" Miss Ritchie smiled.

The boy turned to Marty with a sheepish, self-conscious grin. "Ya. I guess so."

They left the bungalow. "You didn't try very hard in arithmetic today," Marty said as they walked toward their class line. The boy shrugged. "Did you eat breakfast?"

"Ya," he replied awkwardly. "Mama, she make me eat even when I don' want nothin'."

"What time did you go to bed last night?"

"I don' know. My brother, he drink beer last night. He say he be the daddy and play with hisself and piss on the bed and laugh. He do that when he drink. It smell bad." Willy looked up at his teacher.

"How old is he?" Marty asked, his eyes fastened on the child's.

"Fourteen. I don' sleep when he do that."

"Why do your parents let him?"

"Mama, she be at work."

"And your father?"

Willy hesitated.

"Tell your brother to pee in his own bed."

"That his bed. We has two beds and Mama she sleep on one."

"Two in the same bed?"

"Four."

"Four of you?"

"Ya."

IV

When the thirty-seven fifth graders reached Room Six, laughter erupted and the restless children ran around the small second grade chairs and tables, pushing and shouting. Some sat down on the little chairs, but their knees would not fit under the tables. There was momentary bedlam before Marty could settle them to a reading lesson.

Each day Marty was becoming more aware of the barrier these children faced. There was no tradition of learning in their homes, no pattern of discipline he could count on, no visible sense of the importance of school. Each child seemed to survive in whatever way possible but with no basis for confidence in class. His job was to see that they learned, that they somehow achieved.

As the end of the hour approached, Marty had the children close their books and put their heads down. He could not continue the day as though nothing had happened. The pressure in him weighed like a rock. As a high school student, he had experienced the same feeling before track meets, except that with the sound of the gun, the tension vanished. But at this school he had found no such release.

"Why are we using Mrs. Starr's second grade room?" He glanced over the silent, uncomprehending faces. "Last weekend someone damaged your room. Whoever did it thought they were getting my room, but it's not mine. You are the ones who need a place to study." He paused, searching their mute expressions for some sign of understanding. The strain was nearly unbearable. "Your mothers and fathers pay for your classroom with their taxes. Whoever made the mess in your room, is taking something away from you. If you know who did it, I want you to tell me."

"Willy Brown, he know who do it!" Eula Mae blurted out, pointing to her classmate at the front of the room. But quickly she covered her mouth as Willy leapt to his feet, his chair banging against the floor behind him.

The boy's cheeks flared with hot tears. "I kill you, girl!" he cried out.

"William!" Marty shouted.

"I goin' get you, girl!" He glared across at the skinny child, menacing her with all his frustrated might. But Marty moved toward the boy, and Willy grabbed his chair and sat down.

"Every time your room is smashed and broken, it's the same as someone going into your house and stealing your money. Would you like that?"

"My mama, she don' let no stranger in!" one of the girls said indignantly.

"You bet she won't!" Marty replied. "When you're as big as your mothers and fathers you want to be strong so no one takes away what is yours. That's why you go to school. Learning gives you strength, something no one can take away. In school you can make yourself somebody!"

But the noon bell rang, and a murmur spread through class. The children's attention was gone. All that mattered now was to get to the cafeteria and be first on the field for games. Marty walked to the center of the room. "Willy and Eula Mae, stay in your seats."

"When you line up quietly we'll go to lunch," he said to the class. He pointed to a group near the front. "This table." Six children filed toward the two doors, the girls going to one side, the boys to the other.

Release one table at a time. Slow everything down. It was his way to prevent the fights and tears that occurred whenever they were left to themselves.

He pointed to another table. As the children walked toward the doors, someone bumped someone else and a shove was returned. At once Marty motioned them back to their seats. There was an immediate uproar. "If you don't want lunch today, Claiborne," he shouted over the din to the boy who had bumped the girl next to him, "we can all do more arithmetic." And he went to the desk as though to prepare a lesson. The children quickly sat down, watching their teacher. Outside the closed door, there was shouting and pushing in the hallway where youngsters rushed to get to the cafeteria. Next year some would be fifth graders. Marty glanced at the clock. A feeling of utter fatigue came over him.

"All right," he said to the hushed class, "we'll start again. The girls at the front table." He called out one group at a time until they stood in long, silent lines. Before he could walk to the door, someone laughed aloud because someone else was standing on the foot of another and the child did not dare to protest.

Marty shot a glance at Jessie Say, the largest girl in the class, and she quickly moved her foot. "There's not room enough for you without stepping on people?" He wanted to shake her, but instead he motioned them back to their seats. They had to realize he meant what he said. But he must get them outside or there would be no time for lunch. Today he had noon duty.

After dismissing the class, Marty called Eula Mae to his desk. The skinny girl approached expectantly. Her fresh expression contradicted the tattered clothing she wore, today an oversized red sweater with holes in the elbows.

"Did you break into our classroom last weekend?"

The child's eyes opened wide in astonishment. "Oh, no, Mista Hatton!"

"Then how do you know so much about who was there?"

"Valery, she tell me."

"That's a lie, girl!" Willy exploded from his chair. "Valery, she don' know nothin'!"

"Sit down," Marty replied. "Eula Mae gets her turn, then you can talk."

"Valery, she tell me, Mista Hatton."

"Who is Valery?"

"She go to the junior high."

"She ain't never told the truth, no how!" Willy insisted.

"So you weren't at the break-in, Eula Mae?"

"Oh, no, Mista Hatton!"

"Then you don't know who was there."

The child winced, a look of puzzlement clouding her eyes. "But Willy, he do. Valery, she say he do."

"But you don't know that, do you," Marty replied firmly.

"No, Mista Hatton."

"Then why do you blame Willy?"

She hesitated, her lips trembling. "I ain't blame Willy, Mista Hatton." Tears began to form in her expressive eyes.

Marty turned to the papers in front of him. "Don't tell any more tales. You hear me?"

"Oh, yes, Mista Hatton."

"Now go on to the cafeteria before it closes."

"I ain't eatin' in the cafeteria, Mista Hatton."

"Then get your lunch. I want to talk to Willy."

"I ain't got no lunch. Mama, she forget."

"What will you eat?"

"I find something."

Marty took some change from his pocket. "Is that enough for a tray?" She counted the money. "A tray with milk?"

She counted again to be sure. "Yes, Mista Hatton. Thank you, Mista Hatton!" She turned to leave.

"Aren't you going to say something to Willy?"

"Thank you, Willy!" She ran across the room. "But I's sure Valery tell me. Bye, Mista Hatton! Bye, Willy!" She disappeared through the door.

"We've got to hurry," Marty said. "I have duty in ten minutes."

The door flew open and the skinny girl leaned cautiously in. "Mama, she pay you tomorrow, Mista Hatton!" Marty nodded and the door finally closed.

"Do you want to tell me something, Willy?"

"I ain't got nothin' to tell, Mista Hatton." The boy looked up. "My brother, he know who do it. But he ain't say nothin' to me. He be hangin' out somewhere an' have plenty trouble. He tell me he have to watch his back."

"Where does he hang out?"

"I don' know. Mama, she say she be trustin' me to do good, Mista Hatton. I don' tell her nothin' o' his trouble." The child's eyes welled up with tears. "Mama, she get mad. She tell me she have plenty trouble herself. I don' like it when Mama cry, Mista Hatton." He wiped his tears. "Mama, she tell me to stay clear o' him. I wants to run away because o' what Mama do when she find out."

"Listen to your mother, Willy. Do good work, like that paragraph you wrote. You described a bird, remember? You described a bird in the sky as if you were that bird, free and flying through the air. When you do good work like that, you make your mother proud. You can help her forget the trouble she has."

The boy leaned forward, his eyes full of emotion. "I dream last night, Mista Hatton. I dream I was on the street and everybody be pokin' sticks at me. I run to tell Mama. But when I's goin' up the steps by the front door, I turns into a leaf and floats away."

V

Casey Church and Odessa had noon duty with Marty that day. Church, stolid and unmoving, shared the playground with Marty while Odessa covered the area near the cafeteria where the girls played hopscotch and tetherball. Marty walked out to the baseball diamond and watched from behind first base with several of his boys who were waiting a turn to get in the game. He was thinking of Willy when a foul ball raced past, scuffing his shoe. To Marty's surprise, Claiborne quickly bent over and wiped the shoe clean. The boy stood up and grinned broadly at his teacher. "He swinging late, Mista Hatton. He don' do that on purpose."

A surge of emotion caught Marty by surprise. "You're right," he replied and wanted to hug the boy but instead squatted beside him. "When the pitch is thrown," he pointed to the batter, "watch his eyes. Just a blink. That's all it takes to lose the ball. Then it doesn't matter how hard he swings." The next pitch was delivered and another foul ball came their way. "See him flinch?"

"Not watching the ball!" Claiborne recognized with excitement. Marty moved on to the far fence where a sockball game was underway. The girls always played better with a teacher present, but at the moment he gave them little attention.

Willy's agitated eyes haunted Marty, and he turned toward the distant Hollywood Hills. If only Willy could make the leap to that neighborhood of scrub jays and pungent black sage and California quail where he had lived as a youngster, where the noise, the litter from too many people did not exist. Home had been at the top of a canyon where he roamed the hillsides of flowering yucca with his dog and no one bothered them. The outlook was magnificent, but the city below changed over the years—lush tree tops gradually disappeared beneath a brown layer of man-made smog as Los Angeles grew more and more crowded. Now he was inside that murky world. Today, however, Santa Ana winds swept the city clean, the sky overhead was blue and the tall palms behind the fence swayed while clamorous children mirrored the gusty day.

A commotion had begun across the playground. By the time Marty noticed, a dark mass of children was swarming over the open surface toward the heat of action like bees protecting a hive. Marty bolted after them, running across the flat asphalt plain, the faded lines of foursquare and dodgeball blurring underfoot as everyone rushed to the fray. Even the idle ones—those sitting on benches who never played, the laggards at the water fountains, those who loitered in the background waiting for an opportunity to leave their areas—all were released in a tumult of vitality as they threw themselves into the dense, choking rhythm that commingled, that crushed upon the invisible circle where two youngsters slugged it out.

"Back to your areas!" Marty shouted into the throbbing din as he penetrated the territory they were quickly claiming in their sheer mass of numbers. Children hollered in excitement as he passed by, some tried to move, others turned. No one could see the fight, but as a body they instinctively pressed toward the movement that compelled them. The usual boredom that hung over their youthful faces was gone. Excitement flamed and grew to a momentary life of its own until the underlying pulse seemed to come from the very fiber of each child's being.

He caught sight of Casey Church who was standing impassively in the midst of the outrageous discord, his flabby jowls limp while children from every corner of the playground swarmed past. "Y'all belong in the jungle!" he bellowed as Marty raced by. But his shouts were lost in the movement that pressed tighter, blotting a whole section of the flat, hard expanse.

Odessa was in the distance walking straight toward the main building. She would notify the principal who would ring for the big, black custodian, and between the two of them, with the help of Casey Church's wide-set shoulders, they would somehow dispel the fray and find someone to punish, some one child who defied or laughed aloud at them, a child to grab and take to the office so the others would know Mr. D. meant business.

Marty feared the combatants would not be there by the time he arrived. He had seen it before. The guilty ones were sheltered by the masses who idolized them for their defiance, for the aggression of it all, and protected them from discovery with unfaltering finesse. Their strategy would spread with unspoken understanding while Mr. D., the custodian, and Casey Church approached. The children would fall back, move submissively, allow a path to the center. And when the core of the hive was exposed, it would be as hollow as the cries for order—with no sign of a fight. They would intertwine their arms and dance away. And always there would be smiles that glowed with unconscious derision. The men would turn in frustration, as angry for the inconvenience as for the overwhelming feeling of helplessness that mocked their profession.

But on this day Marty Hatton entered the heat of their movement unseen, before the communion of purpose had solidified and established sanctuary for the combatants. The primitive pecking order was not yet formed when he burst through the tight ring that ensconced two small, angry boys who flailed at each other with passionate conviction. He stood beside them for a brief moment, and then they stopped, their eyes wild with dismay. Marty took the two by the arm in the midst of the swarming tumult. "Back to your areas!" he shouted.

As quickly as instinct had brought life to the children, their vitality was gone. The graceful movement faded into lame protests that accompanied Marty and the two boys as they walked to a bench. Some lingered but the teacher ignored them and soon most of the children drifted away.

Marty sat the boys down. Willy Brown stared at the asphalt. He would not face his teacher. Sterling was a plucky fourth grader. "Who started the fight?" Marty asked.

"I ain't hit nobody!" Sterling protested, his lower lip extended in a sullen pout. *It ain't nothin' to do with you!* his resentful eyes insisted.

"Sterling, I was standing beside you," Marty snapped. "Why did you hit William?"

"Uh-uh," came the emphatic denial. The child turned to Willy as tears began to form. "I weren't do nothin' to him. Ya, he hit me!"

"Who started the fight, William?"

Willy looked up, past the children on the playground, as if struggling with something. His anger seemed to dissolve under Marty's intent gaze. "I did!" he blurted.

"Good boy," Marty replied softly to him.

"Man, you crazy!" came from the onlookers.

"Back to your areas!" Marty snapped. Willy's tiny adversary looked at him in stunned silence. "Why did you hit him?" Marty asked.

"He call me nigger boy."

"I ain't call nobody nothin'!" Sterling burst out. "I just mindin' my own business. Ya, an' he hit me!"

"I hear him say it," came from someone in a group of girls.

The small fourth grader looked straight ahead now, determined not to be there. Marty leaned toward him. "We've got something to talk about, you and I!"

"I ain't got nothin' to talk to you!"

Marty led the boy a few yards away to another bench. "So you called him nigger boy."

"I ain't call him nothin'!" Tears rolled down Sterling's cheeks.

"You were trying to hurt Willy. What would you do if he called you a nigger boy?"

The child looked straight at the teacher. "Nobody call me no nigger!"

"Where were you playing?" He pointed to a kickball game. "Next time someone calls you a name, remember how Willy felt."

"He say I can't pitch straight!"

"Then go practice, Sterling. Show him you can."

Marty returned for Willy but instead found Eula Mae. "Mr. D., he take Willy," she said in a rush of excitement.

"What for?" Marty demanded and started immediately for the office.

"Willy, he be fightin' again," the skinny girl replied, half running to keep up.

"How did he know William was fighting?"

"'Cause I tell him! Willy, he go to the office with Mr. D. and Mr. Church. He look mad."

"Who looked mad?"

"Willy, he look mad."

VI

"I've seen this boy before!" Mr. D. announced with unusual force as Marty entered the office. "Been in here every year! That's you, boy! Nearly drove Mrs. Starr crazy." The principal moved around his huge desk and sat down. "Don't you want school, Brown?" He looked at the boy as though he owned the whole world. Willy stared at the principal without answering.

"I want to speak to you about William," Marty said.

"Can't you speak for yourself, boy?" Mr. D. waved his arm in the direction of a big oak arm chair. "Sit there, boy!"

"I don' want nothin'," Willy replied, his expression vacant and detached.

"Jesus!" the frail man ejaculated. "You're all alike. Tear the place up. Don't care a damn! I've had five years of your kind!" He reached for some papers and began writing. "I know what you're going to say, Hatton. Should have listened to Starr two years ago."

Willy bolted for the door. "Where you going, boy?" the principal thundered as Marty stopped him.

Tears burst from Willy's eyes. "I don' want no school!"

"It's not so simple," Mr. D. replied. "You're through here, Brown. You know what I'm talking about?" He set the pen down. "This boy won't be back, Hatton. Sending him to Reese."

"Reese?"

"I've spoken to the staff. They can handle his type."

"Wait a minute. What's going on?"

"I know this boy." Mr. D. leaned back decisively. "Has no use for school. Should paddle the hell out of him, but what for? Same story, Hatton. Nobody's in charge at home."

"But why are you expelling him?"

Mr. D. sat bolt upright. "For fighting, man! Starr begged me to get rid of him. He'd fall out of his chair. Crumple his papers. Anything not to work. Right, Brown?"

"William's doing his work. On the playground today, he told me he'd started the fight."

"The whole damn school knows he started the fight!"

"But he *admitted* it," Marty insisted, his color rising.

"Look, Hatton, you leave this one to me. Decision's made."

"What decision?"

"Hell, man!" Mr. D. slapped the desk with his open hand. "I'm getting him off your back! Don't you understand?"

"He told the truth today."

"Told the truth!" The agitated man shifted his position. "This is your second month, Hatton. Your first teaching assignment, right? And you're telling me that this …" he broke off, pointing at Willy, "that this one should stay? He refuses to work. Starts fights. Been a problem his whole tenure!"

"He's starting to work in class, and I'm telling you he cooperated today."

"Is fighting cooperation, Mr. Hatton?"

"The fight was settled out there. It's finished, and he admitted starting it. A week ago he would have told me nothing. Today, he told the truth!"

"If his work's so good, you show me!" The principal banged the desk in exasperation. "Show me, I said. One good paper! Bring his work here. Let me see. One good paper, Hatton, and you keep him, damn it all! I'll call Reese myself!"

"The paragraph he wrote with his spelling words was destroyed in the break-in. I can't show you a paper." Marty glanced down at the boy. "He drew pictures today in arithmetic. But I'm not talking about papers," he said with emphasis, "I'm talking about Willy's attitude."

"I want something concrete." Mr D. picked up the pen to write then set it down and began fingering the papers. "Hatton. You're a new teacher, all right? Don't tell me I'm wrong without something to back it up." He looked sharply at Marty through thick lenses. "I've worked with all kinds. Been in the game a long time. I know his type. He belongs in Reese."

Marty turned to the boy. "Come see me before you leave today." Willy stared at the floor. "You don't give up, Willy. You understand me?" Marty walked over to him. "You don't give up!" But the child would not respond.

Mr. D. muttered aloud as he resumed writing, "Have to give those who can learn a chance, boy."

VII

"One, two! Button my shoe! Three, four! Shut the door! Five, six! Pick up sticks!" Physical education was their reward when the spelling lesson after lunch had gone well. But before Marty would let the children play games, they did a routine of exercises to warm up. It gave them a chance to shout in unison with all their exuberant might, the one time of day they could show off as a class.

Marty led them vigorously on the playground that afternoon though his mind was reeling at his own ineptitude. His efforts had all gone wrong and now there was nowhere to turn. Willy's trust was shattered. Marty didn't know Reese. The boy would learn something there. That was certain. But what would he learn? *He has to be in school,* Marty thought to himself. *Where else but school will good behavior be rewarded?* Not on the streets. Not even at home for some of them.

When class ended that afternoon, the young teacher went to his bungalow. The workmen were gone for the day but the floor was clean and the broken glass had been replaced. He arranged the day's work on his desk and glanced at his watch. He must find a way to talk to Willy.

He had just begun correcting papers when a banging on the open door interrupted him. A stocky, middle-aged woman in bedroom slippers filled the doorway. Silently she glared at Marty with fists clenched at her sides. She wore a soiled housecoat stretched over fleshy thighs.

"Mrs. Brown?" Marty asked expectantly, hoping for a chance to speak with Willy's mother.

"This Eula Mae's room?" the woman replied, raising one fist.

Marty remembered the lunch money. "Yes, ma'am. It's good of you to stop by, but you didn't have to come today."

"That Eula Mae girl know I has work to do, an' Mista teacher, I has to do it today!" She turned brusquely to the empty room. "You ain't keepin' her after school. I wants that chil' home!"

"You're Mrs.… ."

"Eula Mae my foster chil'," she interrupted. "She know she ain't to keep me waitin' all evenin'!"

"But Eula Mae left school ten minutes ago," he replied. "She might be home already."

"How she do? How that girl do in school?"

He opened the roll book and glanced at the top page as if checking her record. "Eula Mae doesn't cause any trouble," he replied and closed the book.

A glint of satisfaction broke through her tense expression. "She do and she get a whippin'. That chil' get a whippin' if she don' do no work!" The woman turned and as abruptly as she had arrived, she was gone.

"What work?" Marty threw out, challenging the empty doorway. "That Eula Mae girl," he responded with desperate mimicry, "honey, she don't know the top of her paper from the bottom!"

When he finally left his desk and walked to the cement landing outside the bungalow, darkness was approaching. The tall palms stood black and still against streaks of orange sky. A helicopter circled the neighborhood, the rotor bleating and a bright spotlight breaking the soft evening twilight as it searched the awakening streets below. *"This school—a country club,"* he mused to himself. A siren went by in the distance. He leaned on the railing and stared across the empty playground, hoping for a gust of cooling wind that would mean the Santa Ana was over. "Balmy evenings in October. Some things don't change." He glanced at his watch. It was after five o'clock. "Where are you, Willy Brown?"

He turned toward the Hollywood Hills but they disappeared at dusk when Los Angeles took on a life of its own. Instead there was the silhouette of telephone wires that crisscrossed in every direction. Standing there he felt himself inside a spider's web, entrapped and isolated from the rest of the world. The beginning of his seventh week in the classroom, and already he was a lifetime away from the innocent city of his youth, sparkling and quiet and peaceful. His view from the hills would never be the same.

Again he glanced at his watch. It was too late for the child to come by. Perhaps tomorrow. He must find a way to talk to Willy. His worst fear was that there would be no tomorrow. The boy would be buried in conflict before he ever had the satisfaction of learning, of doing something good in life, and no one would notice.

Marty entered the hot bungalow and walked to the back and grabbed Willy's jacket off the hook. It was gathering dust and he shook it. If only the future that weighed with uncertainty for the boy could as easily be shaken off. He went toward the closet but changed his mind and flung the jacket back on the hook where it would remain in the open cloakroom, a reminder. There would be other Willies.

Home of the Brave

He had seldom been around poor people. They were different, he could see that, but the two or three individuals he had met were unassuming and if he thought about them he would have said he liked them. Actually, during his twenty-eight years, what contact he had among the poor left little impression. "You want to work with them?" he had been asked with surprise when he accepted the teaching assignment. There was an element of blame in the tone, as if being poor were a matter of choice. Such remarks made him wonder what the poor were really like. It was not until September 1966 with the beginning of the school year and his first adult assignment, when he climbed the wooden staircase of the old brick annex at the Los Angeles County General Hospital, that he would learn for himself.

I

A hush greeted him at the top of the stairs where a small, cement-floored waiting room was crowded with Negro men and cigarette smoke. Some were sitting, but there were few chairs and most were standing. He stopped, briefcase in hand. Some turned cautiously toward the teacher who nodded slightly though he was startled by their dark, unfamiliar faces. His heart began thumping in his ears. The men appeared clumsy in frayed and patched baggy clothes except for one about his own age who not only was younger than the others but wore a shiny shirt with bloused sleeves, tight slacks and a gold earring on one ear. What had he gotten himself into? There was no way to turn back now. He straightened his necktie and unconsciously buttoned his new corduroy jacket. The strange dark faces turned in his direction as he walked by, and he again nodded mechanically, unsure whether to smile. When his eyes met the expressionless stare of the young man with the gold earring, he looked away and then failed to notice an elderly gent who took off his hat as he silently passed by.

At the end of the hallway he entered the room he had been shown the day before and turned on the lights. The building was half a century old though the classroom itself was freshly painted. The walls were bare except for a large map of North America and a chalk board. It overlooked an alley that separated the building from a maintenance yard, part of the hospital complex. He checked for chalk and an eraser and opened the windows to relieve the heat. September was a warm month and a breeze would be welcome but there was noise outside from an air compressor and immediately he closed the window. Those men crowded in the anteroom would soon fill this classroom. His imagination had already put them, his students, on a chain gang. He set a pile of arithmetic tests on the front desk of each row and placed a pointer on the chalk tray, anything to keep moving. He knew that these men had spent the morning filling their eight-hour day with on-the-job training. They were all on public welfare and were beginning his class to review fundamentals for a civil service examination, a test they had to pass in order to be hired for custodian, laundry worker, machinist, or one of the jobs associated with the maintenance of the hospital. Without thinking, he went to the lectern and glanced uncomprehendingly at his notes—in the tension of the moment his own handwriting was unintelligible. For days as he prepared for the class he had thought of nothing else, but now his hands trembled and he drew a silent, deep breath. "A chain gang," he said to himself and tried to think of something else. "Chain gang," he uttered once again. "They could be a prison chain gang." He had not expected the students in his class to be rough and shabby and mean looking.

The classroom door opened abruptly and one of the hospital's social workers entered. He too was a Negro, young and slender, immaculately dressed with a conspicuous gold watch on his wrist and a diamond ring on the little finger of the same hand. The men who had been waiting crowded the hallway behind him. The last three hours of their work day would be in class. The social worker motioned to them and they filed in one by one, sat down, and stared silently ahead. After making a quick count he set the roster on the teacher's desk, left the room and closed the door.

No one was smiling and the grey, freshly painted walls of the classroom seemed to be closing in. The young teacher turned to the board, wrote his name and walked over to the window, anything to get hold of himself. As they stared silently at him, he returned to the lectern and struggled to control an inner feeling of panic. They must not see his fear. As a school boy he had been warned to stay away from their neighborhoods though he never understood why. It did not occur to him to question when someone implied these people would hurt you. Now twenty-two faced him. The suspicion he imagined in their sober, stiffly silent faces convinced him with undeniable force that they neither trusted nor respected him. He wished at that moment he were anywhere but in that classroom.

"Today we're going to do some testing." His mouth was dry as chalk. He picked up the roster, walked again to the window and back as he glanced at it, then walked a second time to the window, trying to calm himself. "First of all, I'll call your names. When you answer, please raise your hands so I can see who you are." He glanced up but in his tension he saw no faces. "If I don't pronounce your name right," he continued, "let me know. I'm slow learning names." He tried to smile.

At first he had difficulty reading the names, but his confidence gradually returned and he began to perceive an individual each time he looked up. He also noticed the men steal a quick glance at one another and sit up when their names were called.

"Mr. Percy."

"Here."

"Mr. Potter."

"Here."

"Mr. Simmons..." and after the last name, he wondered why they sat a little straighter at the sound of their names. It was their only movement during the entire roll call. He turned to his notes. "Gentlemen, I believe you know the rule of this program, but let's go over it again so there is no question." Some of the men shifted their positions uneasily. "The City has told us that if you miss more than two days within a month you are to be dropped from the program. The reason is that there are a lot of people who would like to work at the hospital." There was no requirement to review rules or explain anything, but without considering what he was doing, his instinct was to be frank with them, to treat them the way he would want to be treated. "Remember, if you miss more than two days a month you'll be dropped." There was silence as the men shifted their positions and glanced around the room. "Any question?"

The moment he asked, he regretted it. One hand went up, then another. Why didn't he simply give the test and send them home? He turned to the man with the gold earring whose hand was up first. He could avoid eye contact no longer. "What is your name?"

"John Simmons. You mean if we isn't here two days we's goin' be dropped?"

"You see, Mr. Simmons, each month we start a new attendance sheet." He held up the roster and indicated the small boxes after each name. "Every day you'll initial this sheet, and if more than two boxes are blank at the end of the month, you'll be dropped."

A thin man wearing a stained, wrinkled necktie spoke out in a high-pitched, carefully articulated diction. "You mean every month you begin a new sheet where we could miss one or two days so that we would not be terminated?" He held his hand in the air during the entire time he spoke.

"Ya, man," John Simmons blurted out with frustration, "all I wan' 'o know is how many days I gotta be here!" The men burst into laughter and at once the tension in the room snapped. John Simmons' sheepish smile caused the teacher to smile.

"You can miss two days every four weeks, okay?" He was still smiling when he turned to his notes. "We will take one break half-way through the period. There are no coffee machines in the building so if you want coffee, someone can bring a pot and we'll make our own."

"Ya, man, I talk to the old lady," Simmons volunteered. "She fix us up."

"If we each contribute a dime, class, we can buy some coffee. I'll bring paper cups and sugar and cream. Is that all right? Who'd like to be the treasurer and collect the money and buy the coffee for us?"

There was a momentary silence. "Ya, man, I do that stuff!" John Simmons stood up smiling. "You give me your money, cats," he said rubbing his hands together. There was an outburst of laughter.

"You ain't goin' take no money o' mine, man," Potter said and reached into his pocket. "You's goin' spend all that money and say you lose it!" There was more laughter, and Simmons faced the group with a big boyish grin.

The teacher felt unexpected relief as he glanced over their expressive faces. "Who would like to help Mr. Simmons?" He handed John Simmons a dime of his own.

"Man, I keep my eye on that cat." Potter stood up.

"Come on, cats," Simmons began, "where's your money? Don't you give me no dollar. Man, this cat's rich. Look a' that! Percy, why you give me that dollar?" Laughter again erupted. "Man, you buy all the coffee!" He stood before the elderly gent who had taken his hat off to the teacher and was now unsure what to do with his crumpled dollar bill. "Percy, you got change, man?"

The money was collected and the teacher again faced the class. "Gentlemen, I have to see how much arithmetic you remember so I know where to begin the lessons." He was relaxed and his voice came easily now as he passed the test papers down each row. "The test starts with addition. Do as many problems as you can and take your time. Some of the problems are hard and I don't expect you to be able to do them all. Let's not have any talking during the test. A man can't do his best work if his neighbor keeps distracting him."

Several men lit cigarettes and hunched over uncomfortably, the papers gathered in close to their chests. One of the big men raised his hand. "You…you wants me to write on this paper?" he asked shyly.

The teacher went over to him. "Put your name on the line." He pointed to the top of the sheet. "See here, where it says 'Name'?" and he waited for the man to laboriously print with large letters his name on the page: JOHN WESLEY. "Now, Mr. Wesley, put your answer under each problem."

He circulated around the room. The man who had tried to give Simmons the dollar bill was sitting at the back watching him, his test sheet blank except for the name 'PERCY' scrawled in big letters across the top. "What's the problem, Mr. Percy?" he asked quietly.

"Well, I don' have my glasses today and can't see so good. I forget about the school. Maybe I do it tomorrow."

"Can you read these numbers?" the teacher inquired. "What is this?"

"Das a five."

"And this?"

"A three."

"Right," he replied and waited. They both stared at the paper.

Then the old man turned to him. "What I supposed to do?"

The teacher was startled. He pointed to the word 'Addition' printed in bold letters at the top of the page. It never occurred to him that they might not know the meaning of a word he considered ordinary. "See what this says? Even if the word *addition* weren't here, whenever you see numbers written with this sign next to them," and he pointed out the plus sign by the first problem, "that means *add*. When you see it, you say to yourself, 'how much is…'" and he read the numbers of the first problem, "'five and three?'"

"I wonder what that little thing mean."

"How much is five and three?"

"It's eight."

"Write eight under the line." Percy wrote a big bold "8". "Now do as many as you can. If your eyes get tired, stop and rest."

"I can do it now. Thank you, suh."

They finished the test that day, and unexpected laughter punctuated the days that followed as the class settled into reviewing basic arithmetic and writing short reports from reading assignments. The teacher no longer reacted to their frowning stares—they no longer seemed a threatening gang. Writing was hard work. It required concentration. But they helped one another and would tease at every opportunity. The discomfort of the crowded room was aggravated by the shop air compressor which never stopped cycling off and then on throughout the afternoon. But whenever the heat became oppressive, the teacher gave them a written assignment and threw open the windows. The noise made it impossible to teach, and even with the windows open the room could be unbearably warm.

During those long afternoons, the teacher would sometimes stare out over the city where the El Sereno Hills separated South Pasadena from the downtown area. The hospital overlooked a wide, flat basin of railroad tracks that led from Union Station. Industry in the area belched waste through tall smoke stacks until the view was obscured and stung his eyes against a bright September sky. The community beyond the tracks where he lived was not visible. He and his neighbors occupied a different world—a world in which school was a place for children. Any contact with Boyle

Heights or South Central was unthinkable. In fact, for most of the people he knew the inner city did not exist. But now he was a teacher and suddenly the worlds overlapped. Yet from where he now stood, at the heart of the populous Los Angeles basin, it was becoming clear to him that the men in this classroom were little different from those who lived in outlying communities, except, of course, they were black and they were poor. But the more acquainted he became with them the more such differences seemed of little significance.

One day at the lectern he stood with papers to correct but was unable to concentrate. An occasional curl of cigarette smoke rose from the tin ashtrays spread among the desks. He moved toward the back of the nearly full classroom, checking to see if anyone needed help. The men no longer registered in his mind as poor or black. What he saw were adults struggling with problems he had mastered in the Fourth Grade. Percy's stooped shoulders looked as if they had done a lot of work, but if it had been unpleasant the calm expression in his eyes gave no indication. With thick, short-cropped grey hair he was always neat. He was also at fifty-seven the oldest in the group and while he didn't speak much he readily laughed at anyone else's humor. He was writing a short report on what he had read about the explorer Coronado. Perspiration was standing out on his temples, and after awhile he pulled off his worn tweed coat and placed it under his hat on the empty chair beside him. He preferred the back row. The teacher continued slowly around the room. It was now incomprehensible to him that these men should be avoided. They made as much effort as anyone to learn and obviously enjoyed one another. Their affection was genuine, and he found their sense of humor not only engaging but completely natural. As he stood at the back, it finally occurred to him why they responded to roll call. Addressing them as "mister" was a title of respect—something new to them, perhaps, but something to feel good about.

The air compressor shut off and the sudden quiet was jarring. He returned to the lectern and noticed that John Wesley had fallen asleep. His first impulse was to awaken the big man, but there was a heavy slumber in his posture—he probably needed the rest. Although he spoke with a stutter, Wesley would not give up on a word that was difficult or a lesson that wasn't clear. He was one of the hard workers, not fast but steady.

Percy looked up when he finished his report on the explorer Coronado. He had not been in a classroom since the year he began working full time.

He was then eleven years old. For forty-six years he had been away from school. To understand a book must be an effort, but he voiced no complaint. The teacher sat down at the desk and asked Percy to read aloud his report on Coronado. Before walking to the front of the class, the old man put on his tweed coat.

"The Coronado Story," he began. "In the spring of 1540 a brave Spaniard set out with a small army to explore the southwestern part of the United States. He search for gold." Nervously he wiped his forehead. "His name was Coronado. After a long time he return to Mexico a tired and disappointed man. For he found no gold. Poor Coronado. What tough luck. Seem like he could have found a couple of bucks." He looked up.

"Where he goin' find a couple o' bucks on the desert, Percy?" John Simmons exclaimed in exasperation. "Man, there ain't no money on the desert!"

"A couple o' bucks ain't a lot," he replied. "Seems he went to a lot o' trouble for nothin'. I figure he deserve somethin' for his trouble." He turned to the teacher.

"That's an example of a figure of speech." The teacher went to the blackboard and wrote A COUPLE OF BUCKS = A LITTLE GOLD. "Mr. Percy wanted to tell us how he felt about Coronado not finding any gold, so instead of repeating 'gold' which he had used already, he said 'a couple of bucks.' That's another way of saying 'a little gold.'"

"That what I mean," Percy responded.

"When you speak you don't use the same word over and over," the teacher concluded. "It's the same when you write."

"Man!" John Simmons was shaking his head. "How you know all that, Percy?"

"I don't know it were good," Percy replied standing erect. "It just something I thought up and put down."

"You can pass your papers up here," the teacher said to the group. "It's time for break." The men left their seats. Someone shook John Wesley, but he continued to slumber. When the room was empty, the teacher went to him. "It's time for break, Mr. Wesley. How about a cup of coffee?"

The big man stirred. His eyes opened with difficulty and rolled around as he tried to focus. "We try hard," he mumbled and stood up. "My wife, she don't read neither." He swayed and the teacher took his arm. The two walked together toward the door. "I dddddddd...dddddddon't know it bbbbbbut we try hard."

Each day the twenty-two black men climbed the creaky wooden stairs of the hospital annex to prepare for the civil service exam. There was seldom an absence because they enjoyed the class with its camaraderie. But more importantly, they wanted work. No one liked being on welfare.

One afternoon as the teacher drove into the hospital complex the large, elaborate wrought iron gate at the entrance caught his attention. The fine workmanship suggested an elegance to the tired hospital facility which gave a false sense of what one would find inside. That gate somehow reminded him of his students—men on welfare dressed in patched and worn clothing, the impression given by their rough speech. However convincing this outer shell, it, too, was false. Little was revealed of the real man. His own sense of them prior to teaching this class had been negative. Yet poor people were seldom in a position to defend themselves.

He drove slowly, looking for a place to park. After eight weeks of study most of the men had learned sufficient spelling and mathematics and developed enough concentration to pass the hospital's exam. But he had no influence beyond the classroom. "If they get past the interview," he wondered to himself, "will they be ready for work?" To be successful they would require something the test did not measure—confidence. "Think on their feet" came to mind. He drove by the maintenance yard and noticed the familiar row of classroom windows along the top of the two-story annex. Could class make a difference? Finally there was a parking space. "Confidence in front of others," he thought to himself as he walked back to the brick building and climbed the familiar stairs.

"Who's ready to test?" he asked aloud as he entered the classroom. A few hands went up tentatively. "You'll have to be more sure than that," was his quick reply. He now had an idea. "This afternoon you're going to review without me." He looked over their ranks for someone to begin the lesson. The men watched intently, wondering what he was talking about. His eyes fixed on a tall, quiet figure sitting along one side.

Potter had missed three days the week before. On the third day the teacher went to the county housing project listed as his address and spoke to a bewildered little woman who said she was his wife. Six small children swarmed around her in the doorway of the nearly empty apartment. Although her speech was halting, he understood that Potter had been arrested. He'd been in a fight but would be released that evening, she hoped. The following day he did return to school and the teacher made certain the social worker excused the absences against him. He could hardly attend class while in jail. Potter was good.

"Mr. Potter, you're the teacher."

Potter stood up grinning so broadly he could not respond. He stared at his desk and seemed embarrassed and pleased at the same time. "I'll put an arithmetic problem on the board," the teacher began. "You explain the problem. Then make up one of your own and call on someone to solve it."

Attention was riveted to the lanky figure who walked up the side aisle. The teacher liked Potter's inner resolve. He not only was the best math student in class, but he gave a sense of authority to all he did. That's probably why he was in a fight. But in class the teacher counted on the others to follow his example.

He wrote out a math problem on the blackboard and handed Potter the chalk. Amid a murmur of chuckles the teacher sat down, faced the front with the others and waited. He knew he was taking a chance.

Potter read the problem then turned to his restless classmates. "Now let's have it quiet in here!" He rapped the chalk firmly on the lectern. "If you goin' learn arithmetic… Simmons, you stop that laughin'. We has a problem on the board here and I goin' explain it to you. And I only goin' do it once. So you listen, 'cause you be doin' one after me."

He pointed to the numbers on the board. "All right. When you see that there sign, that mean add. If you ain't got no sign, then you look at the numbers…"

"You can't say 'ain't', man!" John Simmons blurted out. "Don't you know how to do no talkin'?"

The class burst into laughter. "Excuse me," Potter replied, rapping the chalk to quiet them. "And you raise your hand when you has somethin' to say. You don't jus' interrupt the teacher." He turned back to the board. "Now if there isn't no sign, you look at them numbers. If the top number is smaller, you has to add. If the top number is bigger, then you check if the paper say 'add' or 'subtract.'" He faced the class. "Anybody with a question?" No one responded. "If the top number is smaller, Simmons, how you goin' work the problem?"

"Hell, man, don' call on me. I don' know that shit!" The men roared with delight at Simmons who immediately covered his mouth and glanced at the teacher.

Potter stepped forward. "You don't talk like that when you in class. Now you answer me that question!"

"Well, I can't remember no question, man."

"Well, I ask you again. Now if you sees two numbers like this one, and the top number is smaller and there ain't no…there isn't no sign, how you supposed to do the problem?"

"How's I supposed to know, man? I can't read your mind!"

Tapping his chalk for order, Potter went on unperturbed. "Well, if you was listenin', you wouldn't have to be readin' nobody's mind. But since you wasn't…"

"I was listenin', man. Ask me that question again." Simmons glanced at the teacher with a boyish grin then leaned forward to concentrate as Potter again stated the problem. "Hell, man," Simmons asserted, "you got to add! You think I stupid? You can't work that no way but add!"

Potter looked straight at him. "Why?"

"Why?" Simmons squirmed as he reread the problem, then he sat back a little and stared hard at the numbers. "Why? Why you just look at it, man, and you see why!" he exclaimed, full of confidence. "Don't you ask me no question. How you goin' subtract when you got less on top? Now you answer me that!"

When the laughter subsided, Potter finished the problem and put his own on the board. "Now le' me see," he said, looking over the class. "Simmons."

"I know you's goin' call on me," Simmons moaned. "All right!" he strode with determination to the front. "Give me that chalk, man." Potter handed him the chalk and Simmons stopped where he stood. "Look a' that!" he declared, holding up a tiny piece of chalk and staring at it in disbelief. "If I's goin' work me a problem, I's goin' have me some chalk!" He grabbed a fresh piece from the tray while a few of the men laughed so hard they had difficulty staying in their chairs. He turned to Potter. "Now you sit down!"

Simmons looked at the blackboard a moment then faced the class. His whole frame seemed to wilt under the effort of reading the problem.

"Oh, man, I ain't no teacher!" There was laughter amid protests that he shouldn't say 'ain't'.

"All right!" Simmons turned to the blackboard and worked the problem aloud. "This here seven and…eleven, twelve…" he mumbled as he counted on his fingers. "Sixteen. Put down six and carry one. Nine, ten, and two is twelve. One twenty-six." He hurriedly scribbled the numbers on the board. "Man, I can't read my own writin'!" He rubbed the numbers out with his fist and wrote them again. "Is that right?"

"How do you read the answer?" the teacher asked.

"Man, that's one hundred an' twenty-six."

The teacher smiled with approval. "Is that correct, Mr. Potter?"

"Yes, suh, that's correct."

II

Four more weeks went by and only a few of the original group remained in class. Most had passed the test and were now employed. New people enrolled, including women and Hispanics. For those who had left school prematurely the world was a place of work. The older ones, especially, were grateful to go to school and learn. It was November as the teacher climbed the narrow stairs to the cement-floored foyer, nodded to the secretary, and walked down the hall to his class.

"Good afternoon, ladies," he greeted the early ones who awaited his arrival after their lunch break. Some were already employed at the hospital but were taking his class to pass the exam and become permanent employees. He unlocked the storage cabinet so they could get to their books, and then he sat down at the desk. Each day he would divide the routine math and English lessons with a brief reading in history, something he could use to draw them into discussion.

When he looked up Mrs. Moffett was watching him. She had stacked lumber in Arkansas for fourteen years until her back gave out. But her active, wiry frame offered no clue of past hardship. "I had to do it," she confided one day as she accompanied the teacher across the parking lot on her way to the bus. "It were the only job I could get when my husband quit me with them three kids. That man weren't no good for nothin'. I don't want to live with no man that wake up and call me everything but wife. He left after Josey was born and I ain't heard a word from him since. Sometimes I couldn't make enough, scrubbin' and workin' that yard. Poor Josey, sometimes she don't have no food to eat. That hurt me. I can't stand no child bein' hungry. It make me work harder. An' he be off somewhere. Somewhere to Philadelphia. He never keep no job. That man afraid of the wind."

The teacher nodded from his desk and Mrs. Moffett approached. Though her hair was greying she had the energy and enthusiasm of a young person. "I don' know what to do," she began. "I has to miss class again."

He motioned her to sit down beside the desk. "Things come up," he replied.

"Whew! They sure does. My grandson, he gonna drive me out o' this world. He been in trouble in school and poor Josey, she don't have no time for him 'cause she be workin', so I has to talk to the principal. That boy, he be foolin' with them no good kids an' he be talkin' o' quittin' an' I don't know what to do. He smart! I know he got brains. He got plenty more than Josey got. Lord knows where they come from, but he ain't usin' one! I just don't know what I's goin' do with him. He don' listen. He don' care for nothin'. He just want to be with his friends. He say he goin' get him a job."

"How old is he?"

"He just turn fifteen. He got to go to school one more year an' he don' want to. He don' care if he finish. I talks and talks with that boy. I tells him how hard life goin' be if he don' get no schoolin'. He jus' laugh an' say he don' need no school. He goin' get him a job."

"What does he like to do?"

"He don' do nothin'! He got him an old car an' he always fixin' it somehow. He ain't never satisfied with nothin' but when he work on that car."

"Why don't you bring him here one day for a visit. He can talk with some of the men. Mr. Percy's been around. He knows what it's like to keep a job."

"I tell him to come with me. You's goin' help him. I know you will!"

After break, the teacher assigned a history reading. Mrs. Roan volunteered to read aloud while he left the room to take a telephone call. When he returned she was reading from the text. "…a form of government there as may be to the greatest benefit and comfort of the people, and whereby all injustice, grievances, and oppression may be prevented and kept off as much as possible."

"Who wrote the Ordinance for Virginia, class?" He looked around the room. "Mr. Garcia?"

"The First Virginia Assembly."

"What's important about the First Virginia Assembly?" His question met blank stares. He went over to the map of North America and indicated the Eastern Seaboard. "This part of the New World which wasn't claimed by France or Spain, the English called 'Virginia.' The land was wild and no one knew how big. When the English began to settle in Virginia, there were no cities, no roads, no laws, and all the men had to work hard growing tobacco to make the colony profitable. Remember, Englishmen came to the New World expecting to find gold and make easy money. There was no gold and life turned out to be not so easy. But tobacco was in demand in London and the more they grew, the more profit could be made. Some of the men didn't want to work hard, and they were a problem. If they didn't raise extra food and store it in the summer they would starve in the winter. In 1619 the Corporation in England that sponsored the colony sent over a governor to form a general assembly of landowners to make rules to govern themselves, that is, laws to live by. As Mr. Garcia told us, they were the First Virginia Assembly. What sort of government was that assembly?"

"Oh!" Percy replied. "That was representatives and they was a legislature."

"It was the first representative government in the New World. And it was a legislature. What is the job of a legislature?"

"They makes the law," Mrs. Roan blurted out, then looked embarrassed as though she had made an error.

"A legislature makes laws. That's correct. Do we have a legislature in our government here in the United States?"

"We don' need no legislature," Mrs. Moffett replied.

Everyone was quiet. Percy looked doubtful but took off his old tweed coat and placed it on the empty chair beside him before raising his hand. "We has to have a legislature. Where else we goin' get the laws?"

"We gets the law from the Constitution," Mrs. Moffett declared.

"The Constitution is the main law," the teacher answered, "that's correct. But it doesn't tell us what speed to drive or how much tax to pay. But it does tell us we can make laws to govern ourselves. In fact, it sets up a branch of government to make the laws."

"That's the legislature!" Mrs. Roan responded with enthusiasm.

"I golly," Mrs. Moffett exclaimed, "I never heard that before. You mean we has to make laws besides the Constitution? Whew!"

"Remember when we talked about the government in Washington we said there were three branches," the teacher continued. "Now which one makes the laws?"

"The judge, he make the laws," Simmons replied.

"Let's think about it, Mr. Simmons. If you're driving down the street and you get a ticket and you feel the police made a mistake, that you didn't break the law, who do you go to?"

"To a judge," Percy replied.

"Man, you jus' try it!" Simmons burst out. "That old judge, he laugh you right out o' the place. I try it once, and man, I don't have no chance. That old judge he say, 'Mr. Simmons, you have two violations before for speeding.' I tells him, 'Man, my car, it won't go no fifty miles an hour.'"

"You can't talk to no judge that way," Percy replied, scratching his head in agitation.

"How can I drive fifty if it won't go no fifty? Now, man, you answer me that!" Simmons waved his arms as he spoke and the bloused sleeves flowed with each gesture. "An' then he say some long words an' I still has to pay. He make it less, but I still has to pay. That old judge, man, he don't know nothin'! How my car goin' go no fifty miles an hour? Man, if it would, I'd take the old lady an' drive right out o' here clean gone!" Some of the class broke into laughter. Simmons turned sheepishly to the teacher then at once became serious. "Stop that laughin', Percy!" He waved his arms at the older man. "This here's important. We ain't got no time for you to make no disturbance!"

The teacher pointed to Simmons. "Does the judge make the law when you go in front of him, or does he decide whether you broke the law?"

"He decide if you broke it."

"Then the judge has to know the law. The judge interprets the law or judges. That's where the name comes from. But who makes the law?"

"Congress," Percy suggested.

"What branch of government is the Congress?"

"They's the legislature."

"Right! Congress is the Senators and the Representatives. They make the laws. In 1619 we see the colonists form an assembly to make laws. They were a legislature, and let's keep in mind what they said." The teacher picked up the text. "They wanted a government 'whereby all injustices, grievances, and oppression may be prevented.' Now what else occurred that same year in their colony?" The class was silent. Some of the students looked through the text, trying to find the answer. "What kind of life did they have?"

"They was farmers. They live on plantations."

"And who did the work on the farms?"

"Slaves," Percy replied.

"Not yet, Mr. Percy. Until 1619, the men in the colony did their own work and got work from the Indians when they could. But there was too much for them. They wanted to plant more and more land. More crops meant more profit. But there weren't enough colonists to clear all the land and plow and harvest so at first they purchased Indians captured by neighboring tribes for labor.

"One thing we want to understand is that slavery did not begin with the New World. It was one of the oldest institutions on earth. The ancient Egyptians and Greeks, the Romans and the European tribes all had slaves. So did African tribesmen and American Indians including the Aztec and the Maya. A strong people had slaves. Slavery was a natural result of war and of conquest. Slaves were the defeated people who became the workers. In those days it was believed that captives taken in battle had forfeited their lives and therefore when kept alive could be put to work without any moral concern. To understand slavery, you have to understand the belief that if captured, your life is forfeited. Therefore to be sold into slavery might be something of a relief. At least the individual was still alive and if he could escape and get back to his tribe and live to fight another day, he might, after all, punish his enemy.

"For these colonists the Indians were not a dependable source of labor. They were hunters, don't forget, and they had families out there. They hated manual labor and so would escape into the forest and disappear. They knew the countryside. But what about people from a different land? A different continent? You see, a source of labor was needed, but from what land?"

"Africa?" Percy asked.

"Africa. What do you think happened in the Virginia colony the same year they began a representative government?"

"The slaves come in."

"In 1619, the Dutch sold twenty West African tribesmen to the colonists to be servants for life. The trade was highly profitable and soon the English became part of that trade. In the next century, prominent colonists like John Hancock owned household slaves, and some had ships in the trade. They considered the 'Africa trade,' as they called it, simply another way to turn a profit.

"Eventually, the law was changed to include any children born to their workers because the planters needed labor desperately and these tribesmen from Africa turned out to be a strong, hard working people. Few would run away. America was a strange land to them, don't forget. If they ran away, they had nowhere familiar to go.

"So we see that in 1619, the same year the colonists formed a representative government to improve their way of life and assure their own freedom, they began purchasing tribesmen, who had been captured by neighboring tribes in Africa, as the stronger Indian tribes in the New World did with their neighbors. The world was a different place than we know today."

"My grandma, she work on a plantation," Mrs. Moffett exclaimed. "She come in one night breathless after bein' chased by a white man. She was walkin' home late through the woods an' heard him comin' an' tried to outrun him, but he rode up along side o' her. I was a little girl then but I remember she told me about his beautiful horse."

"Were the laws the same for all the people?"

No one replied. They seemed puzzled as they stared at the teacher. "Sure they was," John Simmons declared flatly.

"Was the Ordinance for Virginia written for all the people?"

"It sure weren't," Mrs. Moffett replied.

"Who was it written for?"

"Them colonists."

"The landowners and merchants in Virginia. They made laws to benefit themselves. But a man in Virginia had to be white and own property in order to vote. If he didn't own property, he couldn't vote. The women in the colony in 1619 were mostly Indians, but what about those African tribesmen brought in to work the fields?"

"The South is no place for black folks to live!" Mrs. Roan shook her head. "When I was ten years old, I remember very well, I didn't have but one pair of shoes and just three dresses. It was in Georgia. My mama, she was a cook for this family and when dinner was served and everybody was through eatin', my mama clear the table and my brother and me would eat the food that was left. We couldn't go in no part of the house. We did all our eatin' in the barn. We was kids an' didn't know no better."

"I'm talking about Louisiana," Percy declared, "when them white boys would come around at night and knock on somebody door and whoever answer they would pull you out and beat you up. They was so bad until my mother an' me would sit in the house with no light an' we was scared if any would show up. Anywhere they would jump on you and beat you up."

"They wasn't the only ones that would beat you up," Mrs. Roan replied. "Because the KKK would walk at night with their hoods on. The next day you would hear that the KK took someone out of their home and whip 'em."

"You sure has to be careful," Mrs. Moffett said. "A cousin o' mine, he had to swim some part of the way over the Mississippi to escape the KK, an' a tugboat pick him up an' carry him to the other side. He couldn't come back home no more. There weren't no freedom for him."

III

Word of the class spread as those who passed the civil service exam were hired by the hospital. Many of the new students were sent by the city's Employment Development Department, while some were part-time hospital employees who sought to become permanent. The class was soon wait-listed. EDD recommended expansion and a second class opened.

The two classes were together for a meeting scheduled by EDD to review changes in hiring procedures at the hospital, but since enough chairs had not been arranged, students stood waiting along the sides and back of the crowded classroom. Those already employed wore white or grey uniforms and old sweaters. Others in drab civilian clothes had been assigned to the class. There were Hispanic faces among the group and a couple of whites, but most were black. The new instructor could not be present though the other teacher was at the back where a few of his men stood.

Ten minutes after the meeting was to begin a tall, striking woman entered the room. The teacher greeted her and directed her to his desk. In manner and appearance she was familiar to him. They could have studied at the same college or been neighbors. She set a new briefcase on the desk. "This is the civil service meeting?" She glanced quickly at him though without waiting for an answer she continued. "Mr. Marion was scheduled to be here but couldn't make it." There was uncertainty in her voice. "I was told to review the application form and explain the importance of the oral interview. Is that what you expect?" She glanced questioningly at the teacher then opened her briefcase and placed a stack of papers on the desk.

"We were told nothing specific," he responded, "only to be here at one o'clock. They'll be grateful for whatever you do."

She searched further in the briefcase and found a pad of notes. "I see," she replied nervously without looking up.

"I'll leave you to it." He joined the men at the back.

Her silver tinted, coiffed hair, gold earrings and tailored suit of glen plaid made an impression and the room hushed. "All right, then." Her voice echoed decision, and she glanced at a gold bracelet which doubled as a wristwatch. "It's late. But I'll begin at the beginning. The interview. When you apply for a civil service job you fill out an I-22. I have some here." Her manicured fingers pressed the stack of papers. "These replace the old I-20. Remember, the application form itself still counts fifteen percent. That hasn't changed. Under the new rulings the oral interview counts forty percent toward your final rating so the impression you make during the interview is very important. I was told to stress that you can pass the written test and not get the job if you have a bad interview."

John Simmons entered the room and seeing his teacher at the back with some of the men, squeezed in next to Percy. "Who's that?" he asked under his breath.

"I don' know," Percy whispered.

"If you have questions," the woman said, looking directly at Simmons, "would you wait until the last ten minutes? I've already begun and I always allow time for questions at the end."

"That's all right, lady," Simmons whispered without humor, "I ain't got no question for you."

"You must be confident when you go to an interview," she continued, regaining her poise. "Remember the interviewer has only a few brief moments to get to know you. You're selling yourself."

"I don' sell myself to nobody," Simmons mumbled and leaned awkwardly against the wall.

"If you don't make a good impression, you have to wait three months, then take the written test again. You go through the whole process a second time. That's standard procedure."

A hand went up.

"Please. I need your cooperation. Save your questions." The student looked around at the teacher then lowered her hand. "It's late," the speaker responded with irritation, "and understand I have a lot to cover. First, you have to sell yourself. Now. How do we go about selling ourselves? Appearance. Appearance is most important." She glanced quickly at her notes. "Men. Men, make sure you have a hair cut and shoes shined. Fingernails clean. Ladies, your hair. Very important. It should be done nicely. Remember, clothes and face presentable. If your sweater has a hole, mend it. And wear some makeup. You'll make a better impression."

"Man!" Simmons let out under his breath, "you sure do recommend yourself most high."

"Next, be friendly. When you're tense, you don't make a good impression." She smiled weakly. "Shake the interviewer's hand. Make an effort. Smile. When you're asked questions, give positive answers. Instead of saying, 'I won't work the graveyard shift,' say, 'I can work the day or swing shifts.' You've given the same information, but the emphasis is changed and the impression is positive. This is very important. There are always more applicants than jobs, so you want to make a good impression..." Again someone's hand went up. "Please. I'll answer questions later. Now..." She turned again to her notes. "Hair cut. Shoes. Did I mention that men should shave? Be sure to shave. Oh, yes. Ladies. No runs in your stockings. You must make a good appearance."

She picked up the stack of papers. "Take one of these. This is the I-22. Remember, fifteen percent. We'll fill it out together. Print neatly with a ballpoint pen. Pencils are not allowed because they can be erased. Very important to have a pen with you. This is normally completed just before the interview." Several hands went up. "No questions, now..."

"Some may not have a pen," the teacher interrupted. "Can they use pencils?"

"Pencils?" She looked startled.

"We ask for pencils in class so they can erase."

"But they're not allowed to erase on the I-22." She fumbled through her briefcase. "I don't have extra pens. They'll spoil the forms if they use pencil."

"We'll consider this practice," the teacher replied.

Each section of the application was then carefully reviewed from beginning to end. The speaker was precise. But the hour ended before she finished and she announced that if there were questions, they should be directed to the teachers.

After dismissal that afternoon there was laughter at the back where some of the men gathered. The teacher approached.

"Oh, it ain't nothin," Percy said with embarrassment. "Simmons, he jus' tellin' a little joke."

"It's an old joke," Simmons admitted. "Papa, he tell me. That lady today, she remind me of it."

"What is it?" the teacher asked.

"I don' know." Simmons hesitated.

"After that hour, I could use a good laugh."

"Oh, man!" Percy took off his tweed jacket and anxiously wiped his forehead.

"Well, if you says so." John Simmons glanced at the others before beginning. "You know, there's this fellow Ike and he a slave in the South." Simmons became animated. "One mornin' his master comes out to the barn where Ike is cleaning things and he says, 'Ike, I certainly did have a strange dream last night.' Ole Ike, he reply, 'Says you did, Massa, says you did? Le' me hear it.' 'All right,' the master says, 'it was like this: I dreamed I went to nigger heaven last night, and saw there a lot of garbage, some old torn down houses, a few old broken-down, rotten fences, the muddiest, sloppiest streets I ever saw, and a big bunch of ragged, dirty niggers walking around.' Well, old Ike, he scratch his head an' look at the master and says, 'Umph, umph, Massa,' an' he shake his head an' he lean on his shovel an' he say, 'You sho must o' et de same thing I do las' night, 'cause I dreamed I went up to de white man's paradise, an' de streets was all o' gold an' silver, an' dey was lots o' milk an' honey, an' pretty pearly gates, but dey wasn't a soul in de whole place!'

The teacher smiled at them uncomfortably though he silently nodded in agreement. "We can learn a lot from that meeting," he responded.

"What went wrong right at the beginning?" The men watched him closely. "When did she arrive?"

"She was late," Percy said.

"And what happens when somebody's late for something important?"

"They gets agitated."

"Right. And then she tried to hide that she felt uneasy, and this made her look like she thought she was better than you. Maybe it was embarrassment. But what you saw made you uncomfortable." The men nodded. "You can make the same mistake with an interviewer. You forget to shave, and the interviewer thinks, 'This guy's lazy. He'll sleep on the job.' In class it's different. We know each other. If Mr. Percy doesn't shave, we know he'll do his work, even if he has to spend extra time to finish it. But how do interviewers know that? They expect you to be like them. If the interviewer didn't shave before the interview, that would mean he didn't care. So if you don't shave, to him it means you don't care."

"That's right," Percy agreed.

"The hospital knows from experience that test scores don't tell everything about a person. They want someone to see you and talk to you before you're hired. She was telling you that what the interviewer sees can be more important than your test score. Remember, the interviewer has no idea who you are as a person."

He turned to Simmons. "Just think, Mr. Simmons, based on what you saw in the meeting, would you hire that woman to be your teacher, even if she passed a written test?"

"No, man!" Simmons responded, and the men laughed and shook their heads in agreement.

"She demonstrated better than we could have planned," the teacher replied.

"That woman, she make a bad interview," Percy concluded.

IV

One day when the teacher arrived earlier than usual, Mrs. Robby was alone in the classroom eating her brown bag lunch. "I know it's coming up to Christmas," the soft-spoken redhead said as he unlocked the metal cabinet, "but I have to be away on Monday. I'm going to see my husband in Camarillo." He returned to the desk and glanced at her with a nod. "I don't like to miss class." Her voice trailed off as he sorted through a stack of papers.

"I've heard of Camarillo, the State mental hospital," he commented without looking up, but his attention was not with her. The last employment test of the year was in a few days and his students were scheduled to take it. The class, although part of a massive anti-poverty program begun under the Kennedy Administration, only today had received word that funding would continue. The calendar on his desk indicated less than three weeks until 1967. He was staring at it with a sense of relief. There would be time in the coming year to prepare those who were not ready for the test. Mrs. Robbie approached. "Forgive me," he said and motioned her to sit down on the chair by his desk.

"I don't want to miss class," she repeated with apprehension. "I take the bus so I spend the night with my girlfriend. But I'll be back for the test."

"Has your husband been there long?"

"Fourteen years, goin' on fifteen. He drank heavy after the war and had a nervous breakdown."

"You think his trouble is from the service?"

"Well, sort of." She fumbled with her purse. "He didn't have no breakdown for eight years, but he just couldn't settle. With all that drinking, I didn't know what to do for him." Her hair was striking though up close strands of grey were visible that crowded the red. She was well past forty and the only white student in class. "I tried to get him into the veterans' hospital here in Los Angeles," she continued, intent on what she was saying, "but the VA doctor said it was nothing to do with the war. Too long ago. I don't understand it. You see, he was on two ships that was torpedoed by the Japanese. He's pretty far gone now. Still thinks he's in the navy and I'm going up to San Francisco to visit him."

"Don't worry about school. Enjoy your visit." The words were out before he realized what he was saying. He wanted to bite his tongue. "What I mean is your husband's more important."

She didn't seem to notice. "At first," she went on, "I couldn't figure why he didn't know where he was. He's sure he's in San Francisco when I come to visit him. But the doctor, he say some of his brain cells are dead, so he can't help it. He don't bother me so much like he used to. I have a boyfriend now and he takes me places. Sometimes my husband get real mad at me for not coming up. He don't understand that I can't afford the bus ticket but once every two months. Welfare don't give me no money to see him. I try to figure some way to pay for the ticket myself. I take it out of food money. My husband thinks I'm working, like during the war when I brought him cigarettes and things. I just can't do it now. I'll be glad when I get hired regular. Then I can go up and see him every month and bring him something. You know, I see a sweater to get him, and I know he'd like it, but I just have to wait. He don't have no one in the world but me. I thought about getting a divorce. Then I thought it wouldn't be right with him all alone. My boyfriend, he'd marry me. But he understands."

Other students arrived and soon class was underway. Jesus Garcia came in late for the third day in a row and promptly fell asleep. He was a confident young Mexican, not yet twenty, who learned quicker than most. During the break, the teacher called him over. "Mr. Garcia, you're going to get me fired coming in late all the time."

"Oh no, mister, I no be late." He sat down by the teacher's desk. "I too sorry to sleep," he lowered his voice, "I got this girl…and she…we might get married. I don't have no sleep for three nights so I sleep at lunch. I tell to my friend to wake me up. But he forget. But he do it."

"She works here?"

"Oh no, mister, she live near me. I know her a couple of weeks. We go out when she come home from work."

"You're in the machine shop?"

"Oh ya," he replied with obvious pride, "machinist's apprentice."

"You don't want to have an accident. Better get some sleep."

"Oh mister, I try last night. But she don't like it. She tell to me, 'Come on, honey. I want to dance!' So I get dressed and we go out. But I tell to her. I tell to her my teacher talk to me. Maybe she listen. I don't know. She like me. But I lose my job if I don't get no sleep."

"Does she have kids?"

"I don't want no kids!"

"Be careful, then."

"Oh no, mister." Again he lowered his voice. "She don't get no kid. She don't come."

"She what?"

"Ya mister. Listen." He leaned forward, confiding significantly. "My buddy, he tell me and it work good for me. She don't come, she don't get no kid."

"You mean she won't get pregnant?"

"Ya mister." He sat back smiling, his plump tummy bulging over a wide leather belt. "It work good for me!"

"Look here." The teacher drew a rough sketch on a piece of paper. "The woman's egg drops down every month. If your sperm gets to it through this little opening, she'll get pregnant. Whether she reaches a climax, whether she comes or not means nothing. It all depends on the time of the month."

"But my buddy, he say…"

"Listen to me. A climax is nice for the woman, but she can have ten kids and never come once in her whole life."

"Oh no, mister!" He stared at the paper. "You sure?"

"There's no question. The woman's egg is there waiting."

"Oh man! Oh man!"

"She should get some protection from her doctor."

"I got to call. Mister, you let me go today and I do all the work you say." He got up from the desk and started toward the door.

"Make an appointment with a doctor."

"Ya mister. I talk to you," and he flew out the door.

A moment later Mrs. Roan entered the classroom. "What happened to Mr. Garcia?" she asked. "He scram like a rabbit down that hall. Look like someone goin' to cut his ears off. Remind me of my brother," she exclaimed and dropped her purse on her chair. "He always try to mold everything his size. Like, one day he goin' raise a fight with me. Mama, she say, 'If you don't be good, Mr. Calvin, the buggerman's goin' to get you and skin you!' You should have seen his face. He run to the barn and hide and Mama, she put me a cup of milk and a biscuit and we start shellin' butter beans for supper. And pretty soon, he come sneakin' in and Mama pretend like she don't see him. And he sit down and start helpin', and Mama, she say, 'You want a biscuit, Mr. Calvin?' And I know everything be fine. But Papa! When he get to drinkin', he whip you for thinkin'!"

"My mama, if I do somethin' she don't like," Mrs. Moffett burst out, "she pull my dress over my head like a sack and she say, 'God make all of us and don't you do nothin' you can't stand up to!' and Mama, she sure give me a whippin'!"

"I'll bet you hollered plenty," the teacher replied.

"I sure do. How you know that?"

"Just a hunch," he responded with a playful grin. "We'd better get started, class. The exam is next week."

V

The hospital complex was quiet even for a Friday as the teacher climbed the creaky wooden staircase for the last meeting before Christmas break. Although everyone had not taken the exam, he agreed they could have a party for the holiday and he had a film to show them. It would give them a treat, he thought, and he planned to dismiss early. To his surprise, the classroom was empty but there was a handwritten message on the blackboard, "Come to room 8."

He walked toward room 8 and recalled the impressions of three months earlier when he had first passed through this same hallway in a state of near terror. He smiled inwardly at his own reaction. Little did he realize at the time that he could not have been with better people.

As he approached, a can of 16mm film under his arm, he wondered why they had moved to a bigger room. The door was locked and he listened before knocking. The women's voices were prominent with Mrs. Roan giving orders. In fact, she had suggested the party.

"Oh, teacher, it's you!" Mrs. Moffett exclaimed as she cracked open the door.

"Well, come on in!" Mrs. Roan's voice rang out. "Supper's almost ready!"

He stared in amazement as the door swung open and two long tables came into view, both covered with colorful paper tablecloths. One was filled with food: a big platter heaped with fried chicken, a huge bowl of freshly cut lettuce topped neatly with slices of tomato, bell pepper, green onions and avocado. There was a plate of carrots and celery and olives, a chocolate cake and a couple of pies. There were three colors of soda pop. On the second table a small Christmas tree was laden with tiny bulbs and surrounded by presents. He stood dumbfounded as the women put out the eating utensils, plates and glasses they had borrowed from the cafeteria where some of them worked.

"We ain't goin' to hurt you," piped Mrs. Moffett's shrill voice. "Come on!" He entered slowly, trying to take it all in.

"What you got there?" Mrs. Moffett asked.

"I'll bet you that's the movie picture he say he goin' show us," Mrs. Roan observed with a grin of satisfaction on her flushed, ebullient face. "Come and smell this here chicken. I know you's goin' like it!"

"Who's been preparing all this food?" he asked in amazement.

"Mrs. Roan," Mrs. Robby replied. "She work all last night cooking. I just make the lemon pie."

"You brought all this on the bus?"

"We sure do. And you goin' like it. I knows you will. First we goin' see your movie picture, then we sit down to eat!"

"You goin' taste my potato pie," Mrs. Moffett exclaimed. "You ain't never had one like it."

"I've never tasted potato pie."

"Why, you in for a treat!"

"You sure is," Mrs. Roan affirmed. "She make it with real butter. It melt in your mouth."

"It sure do. It real good," Mrs. Robby agreed.

The rest of the students arrived and after inviting the second class to join them, the projector was set up and the teacher ran a nature film about beavers that he had borrowed through a friend at Disney studio. He thought it would be a nice diversion for them, something memorable that would make the afternoon special. But now he felt embarrassed as he realized that rather than being the highlight of the afternoon, the film was an interruption of their party more than anything else. Afterwards, as soon as the lights were on, everyone clapped politely then lined up for the food.

Mrs. Roan filled a plate for the teacher, selecting the biggest piece of chicken and the choicest vegetables. Though he had eaten lunch he did not protest. A slice of home baked cake was the most he had expected from their party.

Everyone sat in the big, plain room talking and laughing and eating their fill. The secretary and clerks from the office were invited, and Mrs. Roan gave each a kiss. She was so pleased to have everyone there. The people kidded back and forth. They knew each other either from class or their hospital jobs.

Mrs. Moffett decided it was time to pass out the presents. They had drawn names so that everyone would receive something. No more than a dollar was to be spent for a gift.

Mrs. Roan insisted on presenting the only large gift on the table. She stood in front of everyone, a little out of breath from nerves as she turned to her teacher. "I'm goin' to say it this way," she began. "This is the latest color and I know you goin' like it, because I know how to buy men's clothes. I bought my husband's for twenty-four years. And I don't want you to think we's givin' you no gift to pay you for no teachin'. 'Cause we don't! We's givin' you this out of love. We appreciates you tryin' to stuff our brains with common sense like you do. And you is so patient with me when my brains is locked."

The teacher had no idea, even as she began speaking, that the package would be for him. When he grasped what she was saying, a lump welled up in his throat and he could not utter a word. He accepted the package amid applause and fussed over the wrapping paper, smiling from ear to ear as he fought to hold back tears. But his vision was blurred with moisture that stood in his eyes so he could not focus on the green mohair and wool cardigan he lifted out. He wanted to scold them for spending what money they had on him but at the same time he wished them to know how much they meant to him. It was not the sweater or the party. It was their great affection that touched him most, their generosity to each other, their humor. He had been taught as a youngster to avoid them, but getting to know these people was to care for them. The fear he had brought with him to the classroom was forever gone. He knew that, but still unable to speak, he took off his coat, put on the new cardigan and turned for all to see.

"Why that was made for you!" Mrs. Moffett exclaimed.

"Now I got something to say here," Percy uttered to the teacher's relief and stood up in his old tweed coat and walked to the front. The elderly man with the close-cropped grey hair turned to the group. "First of all, that one is that one!" he exclaimed, shaking his head and pointing to the sweater.

"You pass your test, Percy?" John Simmons interrupted with a pleased glint in his eye.

"I sure do," he replied, "and I go to work on the second day of the new year." The students applauded. "Now I want to honor the teacher—my teacher and my friend. Without this class there would be no job for me." He faced his teacher with embarrassment. "I knows that and I tells my wife that, and she say to me I has to tell you that!" Everyone laughed. "Thank you, suh. Thank you for all the work you put in me. I prays each day to the Almighty that you be full in life, and that you has a long life. I feels it down deep. I means it, suh." There was a murmur of approval.

"Percy," John Simmons broke the silence, "I didn't know you was no preacher."

"I ain't no preacher," he replied firmly. "But I knows when I give thanks for the good in folks."

"How you know that, man?" Simmons chided.

"When your heart tell you, young man, that when you know it."

Soon the party was over and the men carried the dishes back to the cafeteria while the women cleaned the room. "I golly," Mrs. Roan exclaimed, "they eat me out clean gone!"

When the three ladies were ready, the teacher loaded the trunk of his car with empty food containers, serving utensils, the big serving platter and small Christmas tree. He would not let them go home on the bus. The women climbed into his car and together they left the old brick annex and drove into South Central.

Mrs. Moffett was the first to get out. She had wrapped aluminum foil around the plain, paint-chipped posts that supported a second-story balcony and covered it with pine boughs to decorate the front of the duplex where she lived with her daughter and grandson. They all waved good-by to each other.

"She sure have trouble with that grandson," Mrs. Roan said as they rode toward the tiny house she shared with her sister. "And she workin' all the time, tryin' to help Josey keep clothes on that boy's back. He ain't got no appreciation and he don't do nothin' to help. He always in trouble at school. She call me last night cryin' because he weren't home and Josey at work and she sure she have to go to the court today and get him out because he be in trouble again. He come in late, but he weren't in no trouble, thank the Lord."

Finally the teacher and Mrs. Robby were alone. "I live at First and Beaudry for twenty-three years," she explained as she gave directions to her apartment building. "My husband, he used to come into San Diego or San Francisco and I never knew which so I figured I should be in between. It was during the war. We come from Arkansas and I had an uncle here. He's dead now. My boyfriend, he's a butcher. He make good money. He took me dancing for my birthday. We met for dinner. Then we rode the bus up to Hollywood, to the Palladium. We had a good time." She sat in the back seat, staring out the window. In the late afternoon light her red hair faded into a dullish hue.

"My mother, she say to me one day, I remember it well. She say, 'Everybody can't be a sergeant in this life. You can't expect everything to just happen the way you want it.' I wouldn't pay her no mind. I was sure my life was going to be glorious."

CHRISTINA

I

She had missed the afternoon class and was again late to the evening session, but Christina walked the several blocks from the bus stop to school with determination. The night air was cool but invigorating which encouraged her sense of confidence that this evening she would complete at least one assignment. Inside the hallway she shifted her bulky carrier bag from one strong, well-formed shoulder to the other. Before pulling open the heavy door and entering class, she paused to take a deep breath and quietly promise herself that tonight she would make progress toward the diploma.

The classroom was uncomfortably warm and deadly still. "Good evening," she murmured with her soft, high-pitched voice to the teacher. The young woman glanced up but did not reply. Miss Cotton had little patience with students arriving late and Christina made no attempt to explain because she knew Miss Cotton would hear no excuses. Instead she pushed back loose strands of long hair that clung to the sides of her face and crossed to the bookcase under the windows. She was quickly too warm in the heated classroom and felt untidy which, especially in front of the teacher, increased her discomfort. After selecting a math book she walked down the interminable center aisle to the familiar seat at the back.

The overhead lights that hung in a row reflected one by one on her pale, moist cheeks.

She pulled off a sweater, stuffed it behind her on the chair and at once sought the pointed hands of the clock. It was 8:10, later than she thought. She opened a thick folder and skipped past several unfinished assignments. Not finding a particular paper her confidence began to waver, but instead of going through the papers with care, she pulled the crumpled sweater from behind and dropped it onto the back of the chair. After flipping past more papers she finally located the assignment. At first glance the irregular pattern of numbers made no sense and impatiently she again reached for the sweater but this time hung it neatly on the chair. Only then did she read the problem through and try to recall what the teacher had said the night before, but her resolve soon became a ponderous stare.

When she realized Miss Cotton was looking at her, Christina shuddered, took the paper and math text and again walked the long center aisle. Concern with school preoccupied her. In the three months since returning to the classroom she had grown increasingly uncertain. More and more she questioned whether she was capable of earning a high school diploma. The work puzzled her which she had not expected. Every assignment seemed too difficult. But she admired the teacher and when she reached the head of the aisle, her curious, expressive eyes could not help noticing the smart green jacket and fine, cascading earrings prominent beneath the young woman's shiny black hair. Her desk was large and orderly and Christina looked down with quiet longing at Miss Cotton's fingers which at the moment held a red pencil with particular care. She wished she had slender, confident fingers. Her own hands were tired and ordinary.

"You finished the assignment?" The question startled her. "Those problems last night." The woman touched a jeweled fingernail to the tray at the corner of the desk. "Leave them here." Before Christina could reply, Miss Cotton's attention had returned to the paper in front of her.

Christina flushed with embarrassment. She leaned her tall frame slightly forward to confide, "I couldn't finish them."

Her teacher continued to read as though she had not heard. Christina stared at the big desk, unsure of what to do. If only she would explain again, but then Miss Cotton began tapping the desk with the point of her pencil. "You must complete the work yourself," she declared politely but firmly and stopped tapping.

"I know I'm not very smart," Christina replied in a barely audible voice, conscious that she might be disturbing other class members. "Last night. I didn't understand."

"I'm not here to think for you," the young woman declared just above a whisper. "You do remember the problem I solved? Learning means progress. Moving ahead. Classrooms are not static places."

Miss Cotton's ample bosom pressed against the desk as she took the book from Christina's hand, opened it flat and began to write on a piece of scratch paper. The explanation was precise. "First locate the unknown, then isolate it." She explained as she wrote, masking her impatience with a whisper.

"The equal sign separates the numbers from the unknown. You can understand that." She glanced at Christina who stood stark still, scarcely breathing as she attempted to memorize each word the teacher said. "Use the values from the problem. Divide the equation. Both sides. Reduce the answer. The same as yesterday. The very same." She put the paper into the leaves of the text and pushed it across the desk. "If you don't finish this evening," she concluded, "see the teacher at the beginning of class." She took a tissue and carefully lifted tiny beads of perspiration from her finely pointed nose. "And do be on time."

When Christina at last settled into the chair at the back of the room she was in a turmoil. "My brain is no good," she declared to herself as she stared at the long center aisle and wanted to leave the classroom, go away, anywhere, not to open another book, not to be slow and ignorant in front of others. "It's my fault," she accused herself. She knew the teacher was smart. She blamed herself for not remembering, for not asking the question properly, for not finishing high school in the first place. But she could not give up now. The diploma was too important to her. Returning to school had been a recurring dream through years of work. "I must try harder!"

A twinge of life stirred in the heaviness of her expression and she turned to her favorite part of the room. She had missed the sunset that day but now she grew animated while her imagination somehow discovered a glow of warm, fiery color. Each afternoon she would await those moments when the vibrant, yellow-orange sun slowly descended past the solitary view from her classroom seat into the outside world. With the sun's penetrating spell, Christina entered something larger than the fears and doubts that troubled her world. She stared at the dark panes closing in on her and for a brief moment was transfixed with a vision.

At the beginning of the term, Christina had looked forward to class. Books gave her hope. After years of working, she could now study and learn and eventually earn the diploma she had sacrificed when she left school early. A wooden cabinet, which reminded her of a similar cabinet in her father's study, stood locked at the back. "Always silent as if asleep," crossed her mind. The cabinet was never open although the doors were polished from years of use. The classroom had bare walls, except for the round, white-faced clock and an empty blackboard behind the teacher's desk.

But there were flowers, Miss Cotton's plastic flowers, propped in a dry bowl on the metal file cabinet. Each week the teacher changed the paper beneath them to a fresh color. And there were the students, an elderly Chinaman at the front who was never in a hurry. Across the aisle sat a petite, energetic Cuban. "She doesn't bother the teacher," Christina observed to herself. "She understands the work." But each individual concentrated on a different subject so there was no way to compare. Christina never considered that this was a self-study program, not a regular class. But tonight her imagination lingered on the dark mullioned panes where she watched the swollen sun descend in the distance behind slim shadows. The golden light surrounding them moved across her desk.

At last with a fresh sheet of paper and without recalling a word the teacher had spoken, she began to calculate. It was nearly time for the evening session to end.

II

The following afternoon Christina entered class early and went directly to the bookcase before she realized a stranger was sitting in Miss Cotton's chair. His briefcase was propped open with papers spread in every direction over the large desk. She stared in astonishment until he smiled with an openness that startled her.

She worked alone at the back of the room that day and did not speak with the substitute during the afternoon or evening sessions. The next day she was again startled when he appeared beside her desk and offered to explain the problem she was trying to solve. She immediately stood up but he motioned her to remain seated. She was embarrassed and avoided his eyes. Instead she watched his hands which moved as he spoke. He did not mention the confusion of papers on her desk. When he returned to the front of the class, she found herself looking at him. She liked the sound of his voice.

During the evening session, she finally approached him and asked how to set up an equation. Thought problems were difficult. He motioned her to sit down on a chair he had put beside the desk, and he reviewed the steps in the book and worked examples for her at the blackboard. When she recognized the pattern, he took up her problem and she was able to solve it. She completed the chapter without further help.

The following week he asked to see all her work. She handed him the math book, a grammar text, and her folder of papers. "Miss Cotton wants me to finish these before I start something else." Christina sat beside the desk and watched his eyes move rapidly over her papers and wondered if he had always read books and been a teacher. She noticed that once he was reading, he seemed to think of nothing else.

"You shouldn't begin lessons on clauses until you understand the parts of speech," he commented.

"They're not very neat."

"You're still puzzled by adjectives and adverbs."

"Miss Cotton wants me to move ahead. She thinks I'm smarter than I really am." Christina laughed nervously.

"Understanding and being smart are not the same." He glanced at the textbook. "Sometimes we have too many rules. Learning is not simply a matter of rules. We forget rules. The important thing is concentration. With concentration you can learn anything." He leaned back in the chair. "Have you ever read seriously, Christina? Or do you write things down? Experiences? Thoughts?"

"When I was at school I wrote poems," she admitted. "I could never say exactly what I wanted. My brain doesn't work sometimes, but my feelings are strong."

"Did your teachers encourage you?"

"One teacher back home. I was young then."

"Back home?"

"Near Bergen. A place called Voss. I'm Norwegian."

"You came to Los Angeles?"

"It's almost twenty-five years ago my parents moved. I was eleven and could read English. Papa helped me. He was a teacher. But everyone learns English."

He closed her folder. "I want you to begin with prose fiction where we see how language is used to tell a story, and in a good story to express character and experience. No rules. Poetry is another matter. But read poems if you have spare time." He handed her the folder. "And if you like a particular poem, I want you to share it with me."

The cabinet near her seat remained locked and he had to search the desk for keys. But soon they stood together between the open doors and he read aloud from the titles along the packed shelves. *"Silas Marner. Adventures in Literature. The Great Gatsby."* He shook his head. "Why is this cabinet locked?"

"No one uses it."

"Ethan Frome. Five Stories of Willa Cather." Christina watched intently as he pulled a couple of thick anthologies and glanced through the contents. She liked watching his hands. Books seemed to be familiar friends. "You'll find good poems in these surveys," he commented.

Then he opened a slender volume. "This story is by a California writer. John Steinbeck grew up near San Francisco. When he was a boy he observed the people around him." The substitute articulated slowly, as if thinking aloud. "The young Steinbeck wanted to understand them. Some were different," he continued, "especially the old Indians who lived in his valley. There was a certain tension in their faces. You know how much we can imagine from a person's face."

"Oh, yes," she responded and rubbed her full head of hair.

"Look here," and he rested his hand firmly opposite the title page. "This is a short novel, what we call a novelette. Steinbeck decided the story would take place where he had lived as a boy so he wrote about the Salinas Valley. It was as he describes. His characters are the people he had grown up with—a hard-working man like his own father, one of those old Indians he had been around since boyhood and, of course, a pony. He loved animals. This pony could be very much like one he had ridden as a boy."

He closed the book. "Now who do you think the story would be about? Remember the title, *The Red Pony*." He looked at her, pondering his own question. "The father? Maybe an old Indian? Or someone else? Someone who watches them all, who is himself growing and changing, who perhaps is learning about life?"

"About a boy," she replied with confidence.

He nodded and handed her the slender volume. "Write down the words you look up while you're reading. We'll use them for spelling. And keep a dictionary at your desk."

"Dictionary? But Miss Cotton doesn't want me to start any new books."

He closed the cabinet and turned to her. "If your teacher had taught you everything," he declared with a disarming grin, "what would there be for us to do?"

Christina walked lightly up the center aisle to the bookcase where she found a dictionary. She could hardly wait to begin the story. The next day she wore a skirt to class, which she had never done before.

III

The week passed and Christina completed another algebra chapter. After handing in her paper, she stood at the dark windows by the bookcase and stared into the night. The sun had set without her noticing. Finally she turned, her mind racing with thought, and with uncharacteristic boldness faced the room. The substitute busy, always busy, students absorbed in their work. An empty seat near the front caught her eye. She returned to her desk at the back and began to write.

After filling one page and beginning a second, she looked up and the attractive Cuban, returning from the teacher's desk, faced her in the aisle with a paper in her hand and smiled. Her expression. The sympathy in her eyes. Christina stopped writing. It was as if they were friends, as if they shared something. Then in amazement she suddenly understood and returned the smile. The woman was struggling with her assignment. They were all struggling. She was not alone.

When class ended that evening Christina remained at her desk and it was not until he spoke that she looked up. "You only made one error in math. That's good work. Now correct it before you go ahead."

"Can I ask you something?" she said, her color rising.

"Of course."

"Can I change seats?"

"There are no assigned seats. Suit yourself." He gave her the paper then gathered others and went to the file cabinet.

Christina moved to the empty desk she had noticed at the front. "I began coming to school to earn the diploma. But tonight I discovered something." He glanced up from the file cabinet. "We all need people—just to be around." She rested her hands on the books. "I never realized that before."

"A classroom should be a friendly place." He continued filing their work. "By the way, what do you think of the boy, Jody, in the story?"

"I like him. But this evening. The night. The darkness. Sometimes in the dark, I see people laughing. But the people here …" She hesitated. "I thought I could touch them. I never felt that way before. I don't know how to explain!" She stared at him, her eyes wide with emotion. "There was something in class tonight that reminded me of home. Papa. Papa used to read to me when I was young. He said it was a gift—to be able to read." He looked at her and she turned away. "But about little Jody …" Her voice faltered.

"Jody loves life, don't you think?"

"Oh, yes," she replied but could say no more.

The movement of paper interrupted the stillness as he again filed their work. "I noticed you were late this afternoon."

"I can't help it," she replied, her tone suddenly charged. "Usually it happens when I'm asleep."

"I thought one of the students might give you a ride if you had a poor bus connection."

"It's not the bus," she insisted, her high-pitched voice rising. "It's me. I get very tired. I never know when it will happen." She pressed the back of her head. "It hits me like a hammer."

"You mean headaches?"

"No. I have seizures. I'm epileptic."

He closed the file cabinet and crossed to the desk, staring at the papers in his hand. He sat down and Christina collapsed in the silence. She was ashamed.

"Have the seizures bothered you long?"

His voice, and at once she wanted to tell him everything. "Mother would scold at Papa," she began in a flood of intense feeling. "They were both teachers back home but they couldn't teach here. Papa worked in a warehouse and drove a taxi at night. He was working all the time and

Mother would get so angry she frightened me. One day in school the world began to move away. I still see the hands on the clock turning. Time moving away! That was when it first hit me. Everything went black.

"Afterward the school nurse sat me against the wall. She told me to be still. I was exhausted and wanted some water. I remember she kept staring at me. They were trying to reach Mother. Everyone was staring at me.

"Mother didn't like it that someone in her family. Well, I think they were both a little disappointed. She told Papa how much trouble I had caused."

"Did she help you?"

Christina's face went ashen. "I don't see her. One day she left home and that was the end."

"She what?"

"She said, 'You're bad for people!' That's all. Well, I sat by the front door and waited for Papa. There was nothing else to do. He came home late. At first he wanted to return to Norway but he wasn't strong enough anymore. His back was hurting most of the time. As soon as I found a job, I left school."

"Epilepsy isn't anyone's fault."

"Mother doesn't care!" Christina's face tightened.

"I could see it in her eyes. People don't understand!"

"People don't understand?" He asked quietly. "Does that mean no one tries?"

"Do they try?" She crossed the aisle to his desk. "I know why people get epilepsy!" Her eyes darted across his face. "They know … they know people don't like other people!"

"I've never felt that way," he responded at once. He put some papers in his briefcase and turned back to her. "There's nothing to life but what we make of it."

Christina's expression froze. She turned abruptly, picked up her things and walked towards the door. "Good day," she said in her high-pitched voice and left the room.

IV

Christina lay awake through the night, his words echoing in her head. By early dawn she could remain alone no longer and as the sun broke over the horizon, she boarded a bus. The drone of the diesel engine seemed to her a lonely complaint each time the heavy vehicle lumbered into motion with the morning traffic. The horn blared and the bus jerked to a stop. Christina took hold of the chrome support bar beside the seat, closed her tired eyes, and with the rhythmic lull of continual stopping and starting, became one with the pleading vibration …

> *A stocky woman and young Christina came toward her. The girl's fair hair was long and hung straight about her ears. She stared ahead with lackluster eyes. Another child approached who laughed, and young Christina wanted to move away but the big woman grabbed her smartly and held her in place …*
>
> *Young Christina played with her friends on the way home from school. It was summer and they ran along the grass verge. In the neighborhood of big, wood-framed houses, flowers grew in the windows and her grandmother's home was filled with aromas of soup and warm bread. At the heavy kitchen table polished with wear she ate the midday meal and laughed with her grandfather and never felt alone …*
>
> *Christina did not recognize the stucco houses or children who passed by. In the classroom the youngsters laughed when young Christina read aloud, and they laughed the day she came to school with her hair cut short. She was taller than the others and stood silently waiting to join a hopscotch game. The game finished without her and the other girls skipped around, tugging at each other's jackets. Young Christina's eyes followed them even as they moved away. She was sure they were laughing at her. Christina wanted to comfort the young girl but the big woman again came forward and held the child in place …*

The bus jerked. Christina loosened her grip on the chrome bar as her eyes opened with a start. "Everyone I wanted to be close to," she uttered aloud, "Mother would never understand." She reached for the overhead cord.

V

By late afternoon the sun had disappeared behind a growing overcast. Christina was exhausted and wanted to leave class early though she had a question about the new algebra chapter. While she waited to see the substitute, she went to the wooden cabinet and took out one of the anthologies of verse he had shown her and thumbed through the pages until the portrait of a young woman caught her eye. A lengthy poem followed the picture. When the coffee truck arrived for the dinner break, she remained in her seat at the front, absorbed in the same poem.

"Did you work well this afternoon?" His voice. He seemed to enter her thought without intruding.

"I'm reading a poem," she replied.

"I noticed you were busy, but today I hardly drew breath." He indicated the papers before him as he stood up and walked around the desk. "What is the poem?"

"*Renascence* by Edna St. Vincent Millay."

"Yes," he responded with recognition, "you picked a favorite of mine. Can you imagine she wrote that when she was nineteen years old?"

"She wanted to sleep, but sleep stops life. To be close. To touch people." Christina turned away, her eyes full of emotion. His presence. It was as though he and her whole world could become one. "Last night I wanted to write about being alone. That's all."

"I wonder if it can bring people together," he said, leaning back against the desk. "The pain, I mean. Closer to understanding." He fixed his gaze across the room. "Let's consider the poem and your story as one. Could there be elements in common between Steinbeck's Jody and the poet? Experiences of life, for example. Could these give them a special understanding, a special sensitivity …"

His voice fell silent when their eyes met. Christina was watching him, uncomprehending. "You know," he said apologetically, "I forget to stick to the point sometimes." The last thing he wanted was to undermine her confidence. "About touching people," he recalled, "about being alone. Her poem brought the experience to life, don't you think?"

"Oh, yes!"

"But we have your story to consider." He glanced at the clock. "I want to start you on a report. Tomorrow will be my final day. Your teacher is going to be delighted with your progress."

The color drained from Christina's face. "Miss Cotton's coming back."

"She is coming back, and I'd better get a cup of coffee before the break ends if I'm going to last the evening."

The brightly lit school yard with a coffee truck parked to one side was filled with adults from the night classes who mingled among day school lunch tables placed under broad shade trees. All was an indistinct haze to Christina as she approached—bumpy music from the coffee truck, the din of talk and laughter, the smell of burritos and coffee and cheap tomato soup, the trees isolated by slabs of concrete one from another.

She put a tea bag in a large cup of steaming water and passed by a table spread with cartons of milk, boxes of sugar cubes, ketchup in large jars, tiny packets of salt and pepper and mustard. She dropped a lump of sugar into the tea before reaching the big metal waste containers lined up straight in a row. She liked to think of them as soldiers on duty, but tonight she walked by without noticing and went directly to an empty table at the side. Christina took a sandwich from her purse but accidently knocked over the cup of tea. The steaming liquid spread over the flat surface, reached the edge and drained to the pavement below. "I must get some rest," she said aloud and rewrapped the sandwich. The evening was turning gusty and she walked to the bus stop.

The *Albemarle* advertised VACANCY by a sign nailed to the front door. Dead leaves swirled under a huge tree in the unkept yard where its massive root structure had cracked and lifted the cement walkway. Christina entered the building and followed the narrow hall to the rear. Her single apartment was at the end. Through the open door she recognized a familiar figure sitting on the bed and slumped against the wall. "You've been sleeping, Papa." She hung her sweater on a nail inside the door. "I could hear you in the hall."

The old man's eyes opened when she stepped over his long legs. "You early," he grunted hoarsely and cleared his throat.

"I'm tired tonight." Christina pushed aside a threadbare curtain and pulled the string that hung from a naked light bulb above the kitchen table. The alcove was cramped but immaculately clean. She filled an enamel kettle with water, struck a match to light the gas stove and squeezed her tall, handsome frame into the only chair. "What's the matter, Papa? What's happened?" She reached for a brown tea pot and glanced at her father. The sight of his shrunken frame upset her. Her mind blotted away the spent figure …

A young Christina ran to keep up with her father on the steep, graded roadway. He had been fishing, but now the wind was howling in the fjord. He stopped to lift her to his broad shoulders that they might climb the winding road faster and reach the car before the storm hit ...

The kettle began to boil. Christina switched off the burner and filled the tea pot. "Why won't you stand up to her, Papa?" She took down two heavy mugs, filled one with cold water and carried it as she again stepped over his legs to reach the only window in the apartment. A potted plant rested on the narrow sill and she gave it the water. He had come before after seeing her mother, always to talk. And always he slept without coming to a decision and she would spend the night at the kitchen table. Days would pass before she again slept the night through. He made her remember. He was the only person to be close to, her only link with the past.

He shifted his position. "Nooooooh," rushed from his congested lungs as he drifted off to sleep. "Nooooooh." His head rested awkwardly against the wall.

She leaned on the window sill and fingered the leaves of the solitary plant. That warm feeling she had sensed briefly in class the night before began to well up, when her father would read aloud at home before a fire burning in the grate. There were clean lace curtains with potted flowers on the window sills. One day a letter arrived from his brother in California with the photo of a stucco house and garden where he said they could grow vegetables all year around. Her father began talking about a bigger house. He even suggested she could have her own bedroom.

Finally she sat at the kitchen table, opened *The Red Pony* and wanted to forget—not to live in the past, not to go back, not to long anymore for a comfort that was gone forever.

VI

Thunderclouds accumulated bringing rain during the night. The ground was waterlogged and throughout the morning the sky remained dark and threatening. Christina left the apartment early and walked along avenues lined with tall trees. She wanted to be near big trees and didn't care that there was no particular destination. She sought trees though not for shelter. Trees gave her strength. They quieted her mind.

She had now completed *The Red Pony* but stayed away deliberately from the afternoon class. What could she say to the substitute? How would she ever tell him good-by? She continued to walk.

Electric tension in the air mirrored her own agitated state. But turmoil in the atmosphere did its work. Gradually the enormous buildup of clouds, arrayed by powerful, even currents, conformed into patterns that arched across the sky. Late in the day after the gloomy aspect of the storm, the sun momentarily burst forth beneath puffy cumulus masses to embolden the landscape with burnt umber hues and lengthy shadows. All was lit as if by candlelight. Birds sang with fresh vitality and each tiny creature came to life. The evening's light changed—delicate amber to fragile mauve to a deep riband of red along the horizon. And everywhere life sought a nest as though in answer to nature's will. With darkness, Christina returned to her classroom.

The dinner break was ending when she entered the room. Students had congregated near the door, talking one with another. After a day's work, the evening class was long. A few had gone directly to their seats in hopes of completing an extra assignment before the session ended.

Christina's body ached with tiredness, but she was now determined to speak to the substitute. She went directly to her seat. She must speak with him.

"You don't take something tonight?" Christina looked up with a start as the old Chinaman offered a slight bow. "My name Jin," he said. "I bring you tea?" and he bowed a second time.

"Tea?" she asked in momentary confusion. No one had ever bowed to her before. "Oh, no," she replied in a gentle voice, "I don't want anything." She smiled.

He was a little man, and all she recalled later was the expression of approval in his eyes. "You serious student," he said looking at her closely. "You work. Good! My daughter in China. She good student like you." The substitute entered the room and the Chinaman proceeded with a firm, shuffling step to the teacher's desk.

She gripped the slender book. *You don't know I'm finished!* In a fever of excitement, she watched as the old man bowed to the teacher, sat down by the desk and began talking. *I have to see you!* She could not take her eyes from the Chinaman and was lulled momentarily by his monotone voice, but then she remembered the clock. The pointed hands, moving, always moving. *No!* she suddenly uttered within herself. Everything was echoing together, running back and forth in hopeless disarray. *No!* she wanted to scream. Her hands began to tremble and she gripped the book tighter and sought desperately to focus. She searched for the substitute but there was only a blur at the blackboard while the sound of her own breathing filled her ears. *I must talk to you!* A wave of panic seized her. *Can't you see me waiting?* She tried to find the clock, but everything was now a blur. *No!* her inner voice cried out, but another voice struck. *Bad for people!* The big woman was before her, one thick arm holding the child. Suddenly Christina's head beat violently. *Bad for people! Bad for people!* Her body seized and the book slipped from her cramping fingers. She arched forward. "Book! Book!" cleaved the still classroom and her rigid body crashed to the hardwood floor.

The students leapt to their feet and moved back as the substitute rushed from his desk. He took her head in his hands and held it as her body shook with violent spasms. "She can't help herself!" he said sharply. Then the convulsion released and with a deep shudder her body relaxed. She began to breathe evenly.

"It's over now," he said to the stunned class. "She'll be all right."

Before class ended that evening, the substitute went to the empty day-school office where Christina rested on a cot near the nurse's alcove. Although the room was dimly lit, he noticed a corner of the blanket that covered her was crumpled tightly in one hand. He pulled up a chair and sat beside the cot. "How is your head? You gave it a bad thump."

"I've done that before. My head's pretty hard."

"Mr. Jin asked if he could drive you home when you're ready. I thought you wouldn't mind."

"Thank you." She smiled. "Don't worry about my head. The worst part isn't the fall. It's afterwards. You wake up and want to touch someone to be sure you're still alive. Tonight you were there. I recognized your voice." She turned toward him. "I tried to stop. I didn't want to disappoint you."

"Disappoint me?" he replied with feeling. "Not you. There's no reason to blame yourself. You're doing what you know is right. That's all that matters."

"You remind me of Papa when we were at home," she replied and released the blanket. "He never laughed at me. Mother has returned to Norway. He told me last night. I like to think of him there." She wiped her dry mouth. "We would walk together. Sunset was his favorite time of day. He always wanted to be outside when the day promised a good sunset."

"Last summer I journeyed on a bicycle through Norway," he replied. "I'll never forget the strength of the land. Water thundering down steep hillsides into fjords. Snow and ice at high altitudes and the rain. I took a pounding peddling out of the Setesdal Mountains. Terrific headwinds. There was no letup." She watched his expressive hands in the dim light. "I stopped at a youth hostel near a lake. Yellow wildflowers colored the mountainside as if it were spring. The front yard was a meadow, and it seemed more a fluffy covering than tall grass, the way it moved, softly with the wind. After supper I walked across that meadow and sat on a stone hedge and looked out over the valley waiting for the sunset. Behind me three cows grazed, and behind them the mountain rose sharply, high enough that I had to look up to see the sky. There were wild roses and birch trees. Sunset was very late and there was no sound but the wind."

"I love the wind," she answered, her voice confident, her eyes animated. "Papa would take me on his shoulders, especially when the weather got up. He would talk about school, about the importance of learning. He said his students were not whole until they could read and think for themselves. He made sure they passed their exams." She smiled again. "I think that's why the diploma's important to me. Mother didn't like it when we went out together. Now Papa mumbles to himself and sleeps a lot. It hurts to see him that way."

"I've brought you something, Christina," he said in reply and removed a small book from his pocket. "I want you to have this. It includes the poem you read in class. This was given to me by a favorite teacher many years ago. She told me at the time, and she was very much in earnest, that good writers are not simply for entertainment but primarily, she believed, for those who seek understanding of life. Now this should be yours." She took the book from his hand.

"Last night I realized that no one in the story understood Jody, not even his father. And I realized that all those years I was sick Mother didn't understand. She was afraid. You were right—everyone is not like her. The story helped me to see that. I didn't tell you, but I took the book home a couple of times. I looked forward to the story."

VII

The following Monday when Christina entered the classroom Miss Cotton's hairstyle was changed. Although her jacket was new and bright, the careful luster Christina had admired was no longer there.

"Here are your papers," the teacher greeted her, then looked again with surprise at Christina's plaid skirt and striking appearance.

Christina approached her desk and noticed the new nameplate. It had a gold frame and read MRS. JUSTICE. "Congratulations," she remarked softly.

Mrs. Justice nodded. "I see you understood the algebra."

Christina walked to the bookshelves, picked up a math text and paused by the dictionaries before taking one. She went directly to the desk at the back of the room and arranged her things with care. But when she opened the folder, her eyes sought the empty blackboard where the substitute had stood to work examples for her. She always understood.

The wooden cabinet remained unlocked and she took the slender book from the shelf and stood where they had stood, between the cabinet doors, and opened to the page where he had rested his hand as he first explained. She listened while he spoke to her.

"Christina, what are you doing there?" Her pale cheeks flamed crimson at the sound of the teacher's voice. He no longer was there. "You should be reviewing subordinate clauses. You mustn't forget what you were learning."

She held the book against the folds of her skirt and faced around to the teacher. "First I'll review the parts of speech. But I've been reading a novelette," she explained with quiet dignity. "I'm going to write a report." Mrs. Justice sat perfectly still for a moment. Without uttering a word, she reached for a tissue and carefully blotted her nose.

Christina went to her seat, put the reading book under her purse and without looking again at the teacher, she turned to her work.

About the Author

Frederick Kuri, a native of Los Angeles, is a graduate of the University of Southern California. He was one of twenty-five teachers who implemented Adult Basic Education in the Los Angeles area as a major component of the Kennedy Administration's Antipoverty Program.

CPSIA information can be obtained
at www.ICGtesting.com
Printed in the USA
LVOW12*0236310118
564710LV00007B/47/P